THE MOST DIFFICULT JOURNEY YOU'LL EVER MAKE

The Pilgrim's Progress

A Modernized Christian Classic

by John Bunyan

Introduction and Notes by Tony Jones

Modernized Translation by Robert J. Edmonson, CJ

PARACLETE PRESS

BREWSTER, MASSACHUSETTS

The Most Difficult Journey You'll Ever Make: The Pilgrim's Progress

2006 First Printing

Copyright © 2006 by Paraclete Press Inc.
Notes and Introduction copyright © 2006 by Tony Jones

ISBN 10: 1-55725-464-8
ISBN 13: 978-1-55725-464-1

Unless otherwise indicated, Scripture taken from the Holy Bible, Today's New International Version™ TNIV® Copyright © 2001, 2005 by International Bible Society®. All rights reserved worldwide.

The Scripture marked RSV is from The Holy Bible: Revised Standard Version Copyright © 1946, 1952 by Division of Christian Education of the National Council of the Churches of Christ in the United States of America.

Library of Congress Cataloging-in-Publication Data
Bunyan, John, 1628-1688.
    [Pilgrim's progress]The most difficult journey you'll
    ever make : The pilgrim's progress / by John Bunyan;
    modernized translation by Robert J.Edmonson; intro
    duction and notes by Tony Jones.
        p. cm.
ISBN 1-55725-464-8
1. Christian pilgrims and pilgrimages--Fiction. 2. Christian
life--Fiction. 3. Puritan movements--Fiction.
I. Edmonson, Robert J. II. Jones, Tony, 1968- III. Title.

PR3330.A1 2006
823'.4--dc22
                                                    2006019985
10 9 8 7 6 5 4 3 2 1

Published by Paraclete Press
Brewster, Massachusetts
www.paracletepress.com

Printed in the United States of America

Table of Contents

1 Escaping from the City of Destruction   1

2 Christian and Pliable   6

3 A Dangerous Encounter   15

4 Christian Reaches the Narrow Gate   27

5 At the Interpreter's House   33

6 Christian Loses His Burden
   at the Cross   47

7 The Hill of Difficulty   54

8 The House Beautiful   60

9 The Valley of Humiliation   76

10 The Valley of the Shadow of Death   84

11 Faithful's Testimony   91

12 Talkative Joins the Pilgrims   104

13 Christian and Faithful at Vanity Fair   122

14 Encounter with By-ends and Friends   140

15 By-path Meadow and
Doubting Castle   158

16 The Pilgrims Reach the Delectable
Mountains   171

17 Ignorance and Little-faith   178

18 The Pilgrims Learn a Lesson
the Hard Way   191

19 Hopeful's Testimony   197

20 Christian Talks with Ignorance   210

21 To the Land of Beulah   219

22 The Final Conflict   229

23 A Concluding Warning   239

The Author's Conclusion   241

Pilgrim's Progress Introduction
By Tony Jones

Subtle, it's not. John Bunyan's story, *The Pilgrim's Progress,* is quite frank in its depiction of the Christian life. Written by an imprisoned pastor almost 350 years ago, it still captures the attention with its vivid depictions of the journey of an ordinary Christian man.

The book you hold in your hands is arguably the most-read book in the history of the English language after the Bible—some say it's the most-read book in the history of the world after the Bible. Its appeal is not surprising. It is a compelling and fast-moving story of a man, Christian, who is struggling his way toward heaven, the Celestial City.

But most of all, it is the prime example of Christian allegory. Allegory is a way of figuratively representing something—conveying a higher, often spiritual, meaning through common language or symbols. Bunyan names places and characters after Christian virtues and heinous sins.

The point is, quite simply, that the Christian life is hard. There's no easy passage from the time of one's acceptance of Christ's love to that final, promised, eternal reward of life with God in heaven. At every turn, there are temptations that threaten to steal away Christian's joy and divert him from his goal.

All who follow Christ can find resonance with this story.

The Time and Context

Much great literature and theology comes from times of major transition in the author's world. Augustine wrote his *Confessions* during the sunset of the Roman Empire; Martin Luther nailed the "95 Theses" to the door of the Castle Church in Wittenburg as Germany was leaving the Middle Ages and entering the Modern Era; and Martin Luther King, Jr., wrote his "Letter from the Birmingham Jail" as the United States was undergoing a significant shift in race relations.

Bunyan's *Pilgrim's Progress* is no different in that respect. In the 1640s, Oliver Cromwell led a revolt in England—a civil war that ended with the monarchy defeated, King Charles I beheaded, and Cromwell named the Lord Protector of the country in 1653. Cromwell was a Puritan, like Bunyan, and he closed the official Church of England. However, Cromwell's short rule ended when he died of malaria only five years later.

In 1660, King Charles II was enthroned and he imposed the Covenanticle Act in 1664, which banned all church gatherings that were not part of the Church of England. It was because of this law that Quakers and Puritans, including Pastor John Bunyan, were imprisoned. And it was in this tumultuous political and religious environment that he wrote *The Pilgrim's Progress*.

The story itself is reflective of the faith of its author. Bunyan was a Puritan, the group of Christians in the seventeenth century who wanted to "purify" the church in England of its similarities to Roman Catholicism. As you will see, Bunyan was a strict Calvinist theologically, and he takes jabs at Anglicans, Catholics, Quakers, and Jews in *The Pilgrim's Progress*. But he wasn't among the most radical of the Puritans, for late in his life he argued strongly for an "open table," meaning he thought that Christians of different persuasions should be able to take Communion together.

John Bunyan

Born in 1628, John Bunyan became an apprentice to his father as a tinker—meaning that he repaired things like pots and pans. At age sixteen, he enlisted in the Parliamentary Army, fighting against the king in the civil war. A year later, his best friend was shot and killed by his side; at the time he was convinced that he was saved by God's providential hand.

He returned home to Elstow and got married at age twenty. With his first wife he had four children, the oldest of whom was blind. His wife died in 1655, and four years later he remarried.

During his late twenties, Bunyan had a significant conversion experience. He wrote later that his youth was spent in the sinful ways of swearing and dancing, but by age twenty-nine he was a licensed preacher. What is particularly noteworthy, especially as we read *The Pilgrim's Progress*, is that Bunyan was almost completely uneducated. Truly a self-made man, he knew little of literature except the Bible—but the Bible he knew perfectly.

In 1660, at age thirty-two, Bunyan showed up to preach at his church only to find men waiting with a warrant for his arrest. He was charged with "devilishly and perniciously abstaining from coming to [the official Anglican] Church to hear Divine Service, and for being a common upholder of several unlawful meetings and conventicles, to the great disturbance and distraction of the good subjects of this kingdom, contrary to the laws of our sovereign lord and king."

He was held in the Bedford jail for twelve years because he refused to recant and join the Church of England. During that time he made shoelaces to make a bit of money, and he worried about his family and especially his blind daughter, since they were being cared for by the members of his church. But, most significantly, he wrote several books while in prison. In 1675 he was jailed again, and it was during that imprisonment that he wrote *The Pilgrim's Progress.*

The news of this book leaked out slowly—it was not an instant bestseller. But as time went on, it became extremely popular, and it went through ten printings during Bunyan's life.

John Bunyan died in 1688 at the age of sixty. He was buried in Bunhill Fields Cemetery, and you can still visit his grave today. During his life, Bunyan published dozens of sermons, allegories, poems, and many books, but only *The Pilgrim's Progress* can claim to be the second most widely read book in the history of the English language.

Notes for Reading

As with any classic work written over three centuries ago, you're going to find words and phrases that are unfamiliar, even though this is a modernized translation. Sometimes I'll provide a note that will help you through a difficult place, but chances are that you're going to have to read this book with a dictionary (or computer) by your side.

You'll also have to go back sometimes and reread a section. Don't be afraid to do so.

Finally, chances are that, like the millions of Christians who've read this story, you will find many places in this book that are very moving. You'll be reminded of your own journey with Jesus, or you'll think of a friend or a family member who's had similar struggles. Like John Bunyan, I hope that this work will aid you in prayer, guide your devotion, and, ultimately, bring you closer to Jesus.

From the Author's Apology

And now, before I do put up my pen,
I'll show the profit of my book, and then
Commit both thee and it unto that Hand
That pulls the strong down, and makes weak ones
stand.

This book it chalketh out before thine eyes
The man who seeks the everlasting prize.
It shows you whence he came, whither he goes;
What he leaves undone, also what he does;
It shows you how he runs and runs
Till he unto the gate of glory comes.

It shows, too, who set out for life amain,
As if the lasting crown they would obtain;
Here also you may see the reason why
They lose their labor, and like fools do die.

This book will make a traveler of thee,
If by its counsels thou wilt ruled be:
It will direct thee to the Holy Land,
If thou wilt its directions understand:
Yea, it will make the slothful active be;
The blind also delightful things to see.

Wouldst thou read thyself? Oh, then come hither,
And lay my book, thy head and heart together.

John Bunyan

Bunyan opens his book with a poem. His "apology"—or
the reason he wrote this story—explains that this is a tale
that applies to all men and women, and that it's meant for
your head and your heart. You'll find another poem at the
end.

Chapter One

Escaping from the City of Destruction

As I walked through the wilderness of this world, I came to a place where there was a Den [the Bedford jail, where I was imprisoned for twelve years], and there I lay down to sleep. In a dream I saw a man clothed with rags, standing with his face looking away from his own house, with a Book in his hand and a heavy burden on his back (Psalm 38:4). As I looked, he opened the Book and read in it, and as he read, he was crying and trembling. Not being able to contain himself any longer, he began to grieve, saying, "What shall I do?" (Acts 2:37).

Bunyan introduces us to the story by putting himself in the first person—in other words, the story is about him. He is "Christian"—we find out in chapter eight that his name used to be "Graceless." But he's imagining the story about himself in a dream—a dream he had while he was in jail.

It is by reading the Book—clearly the Bible—that Christian feels a burden on his back. The burden is that of one who has been introduced to the truth, but doesn't yet quite know what to do with it. This burden on his back will play a significant role in the journey ahead.

Still in this condition, he turned and went back to his home, trying as best he could to keep his wife and children from seeing his distress. He couldn't be silent long, however, because his troubles seemed to increase. After a while he began to share with his wife and children what was on his mind. "Oh, my dear wife, and you, the children I love, I'm extremely unsettled by this burden that lies so heavily on my back. And more than this, I'm told that our city is going to be burned with fire from heaven, and that both you and I will come to ruin unless some way can be found for us to escape. I haven't found the way yet."

His family was amazed and didn't believe that what he said was true. They thought that some insanity had taken hold of him. Hoping that sleep would settle his mind, they hurried him off to bed. But the night was as troubling to him as the day, and instead of sleeping, he spent the night sighing and weeping.

When the morning came, his family wanted to know how he was. "Worse and worse," he said. He began talking to them again about his burden and his fears, but they wouldn't listen to him. Their hearts were hardening, and they hoped by such things as harsh words they could jolt this foolishness out of him. Sometimes they would make fun of him, sometimes they would scold him, and sometimes they would neglect him. So he began to spend more time in his room, where he would pray for them and would grieve over his misery. At times he would walk out in the countryside; sometimes he would read, sometimes pray. Days passed.

Then I saw him walking in the fields, reading his Book, as he liked to do, and as he read, he exclaimed, as he had done at the beginning, "What shall I do to be saved?" (Acts 16:30).

He looked in one direction and another, as if he wanted to run; yet he stood still, because (as I understood) he couldn't tell which way to go. Then I saw a person named Evangelist, who came to him and asked, "Why are you shouting?"

Evangelist is the first character we meet, outside of the narrator's family. The word "evangelist" comes from the Greek word meaning "one who brings good news." Here it has the general sense of the person who first shows Christian the way out of his anguish. It also stands for the Gospel writers, Matthew, Mark, Luke, and John, who are often referred to in church history as the "Four Evangelists."

The man answered, "Sir, I understand by this Book in my hand that I'm condemned to die, and after that to come to judgment (Hebrews 9:27). I find that I'm not willing to die, and I'm not ready to come to judgment."

Evangelist said, "Why aren't you willing to die, since this life contains so many evils?"

The man answered, "Because I'm afraid that this burden on my back will sink me lower than the grave, and I'll fall into the depths of hell. And, sir, if I'm not fit to go to prison, I'm not fit to go to judgment, and from there to be executed; and the thought of these things makes me shout."

Then Evangelist said, "If this is your condition, why are you standing still?"

"Because I don't know where to go," he answered.

Then Evangelist gave him a parchment roll on which were written these words: "Run away from the punishment that is coming" (Matthew 3:7). So the man read it and, looking at Evangelist very carefully, he asked, "In which direction must I run?" Evangelist pointed with his finger over a very wide space and asked, "Do you see that narrow gate in the distance?" (Matthew 7:13-14).

The man said, "No."

"Do you see that distant shining light?" Evangelist asked (2 Peter 1:19).

"I think I do," the man replied.

Evangelist continued, "Keep that light in your sight and go directly to it. In this way you will see the gate. When you knock at the gate, you will be told what to do."

So I saw in my dream that the man began to run. Now, he hadn't run far from his own door when his wife and children, becoming aware that he was leaving, began to call out to him to return. But the man put his fingers in his ears and kept running, shouting, "Life! Life! Eternal life!"

So he didn't look behind him, but ran toward the middle of the plain (Genesis 19:17).

Chapter Two

Christian and Pliable

The neighbors also came out to see the man run, and as he ran, some mocked, others threatened, and some called after him to return.

Among those who came out, two were resolved to bring him back, by force if necessary. The name of one was Obstinate, and the name of the other, Pliable.

Here we are introduced to Christian's first two companions on the journey, Obstinate and Pliable. These two would make a good comedy team. The former has a heart as hard as stone and will not be persuaded by Christian's scriptural quotes, while the latter twists whichever way the wind blows.

By this time, the man had gotten a good distance ahead of them. As they pursued him, however, they soon overtook him, and he turned to them asking, "Neighbors, why are you coming after me?"

"To persuade you to come back with us," they answered.

The man replied, "There is no way that that can happen. You live in the City of Destruction, the place where I, also, was born. I see now that it is indeed the City of Destruction, and dying there, sooner or later, you will sink lower than the grave into a place that burns with fire and brimstone. So, good neighbors, be content and go along with me."

"What!" said Obstinate, "and leave our friends and comforts behind us?"

"Yes," said Christian (for that was his name), "because everything you give up isn't worthy to be compared with a little of what I'm seeking to enjoy. If you would like to go along with me and stick to it, you will have the same destiny as I will. For where I'm going there's enough, and to spare. Come then, and test whether my words are true (2 Corinthians 4:18)."

"What are the things you're looking for, since you're leaving everything in the world behind?" asked Obstinate.

"I'm looking," said Christian, "for an inheritance that can never perish, spoil, or fade, one that is kept in heaven and is safe there, to be given at the time appointed to those who persevere in seeking it. Read about it, if you will, in my Book (1 Peter 1:4)."

"Not at all!" said Obstinate. "Away with your Book. Will you go back with us or not?"

"No, I won't," said the other, "because I've put my hand to the plow (Luke 9:62)."

Obstinate turned to Pliable and said, "Come then, neighbor Pliable. Let's turn back and go home without him. There are quite a few of these crazy-headed fools who are wiser in their own eyes than seven people who can reason with them."

Pliable said, "Don't speak insults. If what this good Christian says is true, the things he looks for are better than what we have. My heart is inclined to go with my neighbor."

"What? More fools still?" snorted Obstinate. "Listen to me and go back. Who knows where such a mentally confused person as this will lead you? Go back, go back and be wise!"

Christian then exclaimed, "No! Come with me, Pliable! The things that I spoke of are there to be had, and many more glorious ones besides. If you can't believe me, here, read it in this Book. The truth of what is written in it is all confirmed by the Blood of the One who made it (Hebrews 9:17–21)."

"Well, neighbor Obstinate," said Pliable, "I'm starting to come to a decision. I'm going along with this good man. But, my good companion, do you know the way to this enjoyable place?"

"I'm directed by a person named Evangelist," replied Christian, "to go quickly to a little narrow gate that lies ahead of us, where we will receive instructions about the Way."

"Come then, good neighbor," answered Pliable, "let's be on our way."

So they both went along together.

"And I'll go back to my place," shouted Obstinate over his shoulder. "I won't be the companion of such misled, fanatical people."

I saw in my dream that when Obstinate left, Christian and Pliable went walking over the plain, talking together as they went.

"Come, neighbor Pliable, how are you doing? I'm glad you were persuaded to go along with me. If only Obstinate himself had felt what I've felt of the powers and terrors of what can't be seen yet, he wouldn't have turned his back on us so lightly!"

Pliable replied, "My good neighbor, since there are only the two of us here, tell me more now about the wonderful things where we're going."

"I can conceive them in my mind better than I can put them into words," answered his companion. "But, since you want to know, I'll read about them in my Book (1 Corinthians 2:9)."

"And do you think that the words of your Book are certainly true?" asked Pliable.

"Yes, truly," Christian avowed. "This Book was made by the One who cannot lie (Titus 1:2)."

"Well said! What wonderful things are they?"

"There's an endless kingdom to live in, and everlasting life to be given us, so that we may live in that kingdom forever."

"Well said! And what else?"

"There are crowns of glory to be given us, and clothes that will make us shine like the sun in the heavens (2 Timothy 4:8)."

"This is very pleasant," continued Pliable. "And what else?"

"There will be no more crying, and no sorrow, for the One who is the Owner of the place will wipe away all tears from our eyes (Revelation 22:4)."

"And what company will we have there?" asked Pliable.

"There we will be with angels—seraphim and cherubim (Isaiah 6:2, Revelation 5:11)," answered Christian, "creatures that will dazzle your eyes to look at them. There also you will meet with thousands and tens of thousands who have gone before us to that place. None of them is hurtful, but all are loving and holy; everyone is walking in the sight of God, standing in His presence forever. In a word, we will see the elders with their golden crowns (Revelation 4:4); there we will see the holy virgins with their golden harps (Revelation 14:1–5); there we will see persons who were cut in pieces by the world, burned in flames, eaten by beasts, drowned in the seas—all for the love they bear for the Lord of that place (John 12:25). They will all be well and will be clothed with immortality as with a garment (2 Corinthians 5:2)."

"Hearing this is enough to delight a person's heart!" exclaimed Pliable. "But are these things to be enjoyed? How will we get to share in them?"

"The Lord, the Governor of that country, has recorded all that in this Book," Christian went on. "The substance of it is this: If we are truly willing to have it, He will freely bestow it upon us (Isaiah 55:1)."

"Well, my good companion, I'm glad to hear of these things. Come on, let's increase our pace!"

Christian replied sadly, "I can't go as fast as I would like to because of this burden on my back."

I saw in my dream that just as they ended this talk, they came to a very muddy, slimy swamp in the middle of the plain. Not noticing it, they both fell suddenly into it. It is called the Slough of Despond, meaning "the hollow filled with deep mud and symbolizing discouragement."Here they wallowed for a time, and were seriously covered with dirt and mud. Christian, because of the burden on his back, began to sink into the slimy mud.

Then Pliable called out, "Ah! neighbor Christian, where are you now?"

"To tell you the truth," said Christian, "I don't know."

At this Pliable became offended, and angrily said to his companion, "Is this the happiness you told me of all the way here? If we have such trouble at the beginning of our journey, what can we expect between this and our journey's end? If I get out of this mud alive, you will possess the brave country alone for me."

 The slightest bit of trouble sends Pliable packing—while Christian plows through the quicksand of discouragement, Pliable climbs back out and shouts sarcastically that Christian can get to the Promised Land alone.

And with that, he gave a desperate struggle or two, and got out of the mud on the side of the swamp that was nearest his own house. Away he went, and Christian saw no more of him.

Christian, then, was left to tumble in the Slough of Despond alone. He kept endeavoring to struggle to the side of the Slough farthest from his own house, toward the narrow gate. Yet he couldn't get out of the mud because of the great burden on his back.

But I saw in my dream that a person came to him whose name was Help, and asked him what he was doing there.

"Sir," said Christian, "I was told to go this way by a person called Evangelist, who directed me to that gate over there, so that I might escape the divine punishment that is coming. As I was going, I fell in here."

"But why didn't you look for the steps?" asked the other.

"Fear was following me so closely," said Christian, "that I ran without paying attention, and fell in."

Then Help said, "Give me your hand." So Christian gave Help his hand, and Help pulled Christian out and set him on solid ground and told him to go on his way (Psalm 40:2).

I then approached the one who had pulled Christian out and asked him, "Sir, since this is the route from the City of Destruction to that gate over there, why is it that this area isn't repaired, so that poor travelers might go over it more safely?"

He replied, "This muddy hollow is the type of place that can't be repaired. It's the descent where the scum and filth that accompany the conviction of sin continually run, and therefore it's called the Slough of Despond. For still, as the sinner wakes up and realizes his lost condition, many fears and doubts and discouraging apprehensions arise in his soul. All of them get together and settle in this place. This is the reason for the badness of the ground.

"It is not the pleasure of the King that this place should remain so bad," he went on (Isaiah 35:3). "For about sixteen hundred years His laborers also have, by the direction of His Majesty's surveyors, been employed about this patch of ground, in case it might be able to be repaired. Yes, and to my knowledge," he said, "at least twenty thousand cartloads have been swallowed up here—yes, millions of wholesome instructions that have at all seasons been brought from all kinds of places in the King's dominions (and those who can tell say they are the best materials to make good ground out of the place)—in hopes that it might have been repaired. But it's still the Slough of Despond, and it will continue to be so when they've done all they can.

 Bunyan uses Help to make an important theological point. This Slough of Despond is not on the path because

of God's desire, but because of our condition as human beings. Regardless of the greatness of God and God's salvation, humans on the path to God inevitably struggle with doubt and despondence, and the only way to survive it is to push on through—with God's "Help."

"It's true," he went on, "that there are, by the direction of the Lawgiver, certain good, substantial steps, placed through the very middle of this slough. But at the times when this place spews out its filth, as it does on any change of weather, those steps are hard to see. And even if they are, people, through the dizziness of their heads, miss them and fall into the mud, even though the steps are there. But the ground is good when they've gotten in at the gate (1 Samuel 12:23)."

Now, I saw in my dream that by this time Pliable had arrived back at his home. His neighbors came to visit him, and some of them called him wise for coming back, while others called him a fool for endangering himself with Christian in the first place. Others made fun of his cowardliness, saying, "Surely since you set out on an adventure, I wouldn't have been so selfish and mean-spirited as to quit because of a few difficulties." So Pliable sat shamefacedly among them. But after a while he regained his confidence, and then they all began to ridicule poor Christian behind his back. So much for Pliable.

Chapter Three

A Dangerous Encounter

As Christian was walking along by himself, he caught sight of someone far off, coming across the field to meet him. It happened that they met just as their paths crossed one another. The gentleman's name was Mr. Worldly Wiseman, and he lived in the town of Worldly Policy, a very great town not far from the one from which Christian came. Christian's leaving the City of Destruction had been widely talked about, so that Mr. Worldly Wiseman had heard of him and his journey. Observing Christian's laborious efforts, and hearing his sighs and groans, he spoke to him in this manner:

 Enter stage left: Mr. Worldly Wiseman, one of the more colorful characters in the story. A smooth-talking, used-car-salesman type, he takes Christian on a detour by convincing him that he has to get rid of his burden immediately. Still a little gullible this early in his journey, Christian goes along with Mr. WW—of course, he will find that there is no shortcut for relief from his heavy load.

"Well now, my good man! Where are you going in this burdened manner?"

"A burdened manner indeed, as ever I think any poor creature had," was Christian's response. "And since you ask me where I'm going, I tell you, sir, I'm going to that narrow gate in the distance, where, I've been informed, I'll be enabled to get rid of my heavy burden."

"Do you have a wife and children?" asked the other.

"Yes," said Christian. "But I'm so weighed down with this burden that I can't take pleasure in them as I formerly did. I think I am as though I had no family (1 Corinthians 7:29)."

Mr. Worldly Wiseman looked at him shrewdly, saying, "Will you listen to me if I give you counsel?"

"If it's good, I will," said Christian. "For I'm certainly in need of good counsel."

"I would advise you, then, with all speed to rid yourself of this burden. You will never be settled in your mind until then. Nor can you enjoy the blessings God has bestowed on you till then."

Christian answered, "That's what I'm looking for, namely to be rid of this heavy burden, but I can't get it off myself, nor is there anyone in our country who can take it off my shoulders. I'm going this way, as I told you, in order to get rid of my burden."

"Who told you to go this way to get rid of your burden?" asked the other.

"A person who appeared to me to be a very great and honorable person. His name, as I remember, is Evangelist."

"I curse him for his counsel!" exclaimed Worldly Wiseman. "There is no more dangerous and troublesome way in the world than the one to which he has directed you! You will find this to be the case if you follow his advice! I notice that you have already encountered some difficulty, for I see the dirt of the Slough of Despond is on you. But that slough is only the beginning of sorrows that accompany those who go on in that way. Listen to me! for I am older and wiser than you. In this way you're on, you're likely to meet with weariness, pain, hunger, perils, nakedness, sword, lions, dragons, darkness, and, in a word—death and such things! These things are certainly true, and have been confirmed by many testimonies. Why should a person so carelessly throw himself away by paying attention to a stranger?"

"Why sir," replied Christian, "this burden on my back is more terrible to me than all those things you've mentioned. No! I think I don't care what I encounter on the Way, if only I can also encounter deliverance from my burden."

"How did you come by the burden in the first place?" asked the other.

"By reading this Book in my hand," said Christian.

"I thought so!" retorted Worldly Wiseman. "And it's happened to you just as it has to other weak persons who meddle in things too high for them. They suddenly fall into the same distractions as you have—distractions that not only take away people's courage, but lead them into desperate ventures to obtain something that they know nothing about!"

 Ironically, Mr. WW warns Christian to avoid distractions, even as he himself is being a distraction!

"I know what I want to obtain," Christian replied. "I want to obtain relief from my heavy burden!"

"But why will you seek for relief this way, seeing that so many dangers accompany it? Especially since I could direct you to get what you desire without these dangers that you're going to meet if you continue in this way, if only you had patience to listen to me. Besides," Worldly Wiseman continued, "I'll add that, instead of those dangers, you'll meet with much safety, friendship, and contentment."

"Sir," said Christian hopefully, "I beg you, reveal this secret to me."

Worldly Wiseman proceeded: "In that village over there, called Morality, there lives a gentleman whose name is Legality—a very judicious person, a person of very good reputation. He has skill to help people get rid of such burdens as yours. To my knowledge, he's done a great deal of good in this way. Yes, and besides, he has skill to cure those who are somewhat crazed in their wits with their burdens. As I said, you may go to him and be helped very quickly. His house is not quite a mile from here, and if he isn't at home, he has a son named Civility who can help you quite as well as the old gentleman himself. There you may be relieved of your burden, and if you don't feel like going back to your former home (as indeed I wouldn't want you to do), you may send for your wife and children and find a home in this village at a reasonable rate. Supplies there are cheap and good. What will make your own life even happier is that in this village you're sure to be living among honest neighbors, in credit and good fashion."

The temptation that Worldly Wiseman lays before Christian is to get rid of his burden by means of law (Legality) and right living (Civility) in the town of Morality. But, of course, a person cannot be saved by the law or by living a good life, and Christian finds the hills to Morality too steep to climb.

Christian was confused by this speech. Soon he concluded, "If what this gentleman has said is true, my wisest course is to take his advice." With that he said, "Sir, which is the way to this honest person's house?"

"Do you see that high hill over there?"

"Yes, very well."

"You must go by that hill," said Worldly Wiseman. "And the first house you come to is his."

So Christian turned out of his way to go to Mr. Legality's house for help. But when he was very close to the hill, it seemed so high, and the side next to him seemed to hang over the road in such a dangerous way, that Christian was afraid to venture farther, for fear that the hill would fall on his head. So he stood still, not knowing what to do. His burden, too, seemed even heavier than before. There also came flashes of lightning out of the hill, so that Christian was afraid he would be burned, and he began to sweat and tremble with fear.

He was sorry now that he had listened to Mr. Worldly Wiseman's advice. While he stood there, not knowing what to do, he saw Evangelist coming toward him. At the sight of him, Christian blushed for shame. Coming up to him, Evangelist looked at him with a severe and dreadful expression, and began to talk with Christian. "What are you doing here, Christian?" he said. Christian didn't know how to answer, so he stood there speechless before him. Evangelist went on, "Aren't you the person that I found shouting outside the City of Destruction?"

 Evangelist returns to the scene, finding Christian at the bottom of Morality cliff. But Evangelist is not lighthearted here—he is stern and dour, scolding Christian for listening to the voice of Worldly Wiseman. Evangelist goes on to use Scripture to show Christian the difference between worldly ways and God's ways.

"Yes, dear sir, I'm the one."

"Didn't I show you the way to the little narrow gate?"

"Yes, dear sir," said Christian.

"How is it then, that you are so quickly turned aside? For you are now out of the Way," said Evangelist.

"I met up with a gentleman soon after I got over the Slough of Despond," explained Christian. "He persuaded me that I might, in this village before me, find a person who could take off my burden."

"What was he?" asked Evangelist.

"He looked like a gentleman, and talked a great deal to me, and got me at last to give in. So I came this way, but when I saw this hill and how it hangs over the road, I stopped for fear that it would fall on my head."

"What did that gentleman say to you?"

"He asked me where I was going, and I told him."

"And what did he say then?" Evangelist persisted.

"He asked me if I had a family, and I told him. 'But,' I said, 'I'm so weighed down with the burden on my back that I can't take pleasure in them as used to do.' "

"And what did he say then?"

Christian answered, "He invited me to get rid of my burden quickly, and I told him this is what I wanted to do. 'And,' I said, 'I'm going to that narrow gate in the distance to receive further direction on how I may get to the place of deliverance.' So he said that he would show me a better and shorter way, not as much accompanied by difficulties as the Way, sir, that you sent me in. 'This way,' he said, 'will direct you to a gentleman's house who has skill to take off these burdens.' So I believed him, and turned out of that Way into this one, hoping that I might soon be relieved of my burden. But when I came to this place, and saw things as they are, I stopped for fear of danger, as I said. Now, I don't know what to do."

Then Evangelist said, "Stand still for a little while, so that I may show you the words of God."

He stood, trembling. Then said Evangelist, "See that you do not refuse the one who speaks; for if they didn't escape when they refused the one who warned them on earth, much less will we, if we turn away from Him who warns us from heaven? (cf. Hebrews 12:25)." And again, "But my righteous will live by faith. And I take no pleasure in the one who shrinks back (Hebrews 10:38)." Then he applied these words like this: "You're running into misery. You've begun to reject the counsel of the Most High, and to draw back from the Way of peace, even almost to the point of your utter ruin."

Christian fell down at his feet as if he were dead, crying, "I'm distressed, because I'm ruined!"

Evangelist caught him by the right hand, saying, "People will be forgiven every sin and blasphemy (Matthew 12:31). Stop doubting and believe

(John 20:27)." Then Christian revived a little, and stood up again, still trembling.

Evangelist then continued, "Pay more earnest attention to the things that I'm going to tell you. I'll show you who has deluded you, and who it was to whom he sent you. The person who met you is named Worldly Wiseman, rightly so called because he likes only the teaching of this world (1 John 4:5). For this reason he always goes to the town of Morality to church. The reason he loves the world's doctrine best is that it saves him from the Cross (Galatians 6:12). Because he is of this worldly or fleshly state of mind, he attempts to pervert my ways, although they are right. There are three things in this person's counsel that you must utterly detest and avoid:

"First, that he turned you out of the Way.

"Second, that he tried to make the Cross hateful to you.

"Third, that he set your feet in that way that leads to death.

"First—you must loathe his turning you out of the Way; yes, and your own agreeing to it, because this is to reject the counsel of God for the sake of the counsel of a worldly wiseman. The Lord says, 'Make every effort to enter through the narrow gate (cf. Luke 13:24),' the gate to which I am sending you; for 'small is the gate and narrow the road that leads to life, and only a few find it' (Matthew 7:14). This wicked person has turned you from this little narrow gate, and from the way to it, bringing you almost to destruction. Therefore, hate his turning you out of the Way, and detest yourself for listening to him.

"Second—you must loathe his efforts to make the Cross hateful to you, because you are to prefer the Cross above all the treasures of Egypt (Hebrews 11:25-26). The King of Glory has told you that anyone who would save their life will lose it, and that a person who comes after Him, and doesn't hate father, mother, wife, children, brothers, and sisters—even life itself, can't be his disciple (Mark 8:38, John 12:25, Matthew 10:39, Luke 14:26). I say, then, for a person to endeavor to persuade you that the very thing will be death to you without which the Truth says you can't have eternal life, this teaching you must loathe and hate.

"Third—you must hate his setting your feet in the way that leads to death. And for this you must consider to whom he sent you and how unable that person is to deliver you from your burden.

"The one to whom you were sent is named Legality, the son of a slave who is now enslaved with her children (Galatians 4:21–27), and this mountain that you were afraid would fall on your head is Mount Sinai. Now if she with her children is in slavery, how can you expect them to free you? Therefore this Legality isn't able to free you from your burden. No one yet was ever rid of their burden due to him, nor is anyone ever likely to be.

Here we get a taste of the anti-Semitism of Bunyan's day. You might have caught it earlier in the temptation to Legality, but here the author makes it abundantly clear that Mt. Sinai (a not-so-subtle reference to the Jewish faith) will fall on the head of anyone who tries to be saved by the Law.

"You can't be justified by the law, for by observing the law no living person can be rid of their burden (Galatians 3:11). Therefore, Mr. Worldly Wiseman is a foreigner and Mr. Legality is a cheat; and as for his son, Civility, notwithstanding his simpering looks, he's only a hypocrite and can't help you. Believe me, there's nothing in all this noise that you've heard from these foolish persons, but a plot to deceive you and cheat you of your salvation by turning you from the Way in which I had set you."

After this, Evangelist called aloud to the heavens for confirmation of what he had said, and with that there came words and fire out of the mountain under which poor Christian stood, and these made the hair of his flesh stand up. These words were pronounced: "All who rely on observing the law are under a curse: for it is written, 'Cursed is everyone who does not continue to do everything written in the book of the law' (Galatians 3:10)."

Now Christian looked for nothing but death, and began to shout and lament, even to curse the time when he met Mr. Worldly Wiseman. He called himself a fool a thousand times over, to think that this gentleman's arguments, flowing only from the flesh, could have won him over so far as to cause him to forsake the right way. This done, he spoke again to Evangelist in words something like this:

"Sir, what do you think? Is there any hope? May I now go back and go up to the narrow gate? Shall I not be abandoned for this, and sent back condemned? I'm sorry that I've listened to this person's counsel. Can my sin be forgiven?"

"Your sin is very great," answered Evangelist, "for by it you have committed two evils: You have forsaken the Way that is good, and you have walked in forbidden paths. Yet the man at the gate will receive you. But be careful not to turn aside again, for fear that you perish from the way, for his wrath can flare up in a moment (Psalm 2:12)."

Christian turned to go back, and Evangelist, when he had embraced him, gave him a smile and wished him success on his journey. So he hurried on. He didn't speak to anyone along the way, and if anyone asked him anything, he didn't give an answer. He went like one who was all the time walking on forbidden ground, and who couldn't consider himself safe till he was once more back in the Way he had left to follow Mr. Worldly Wiseman's counsel. So, in the process of time, Christian got up to the gate.

Christian Reaches the Narrow Gate

Over the narrow gate there was written: "Knock and the door will be opened to you (Matthew 7:7)."

Therefore he knocked, more than once or twice, saying:

May I now enter here? Will He within
Open to sorry me, though I have been
An undeserving rebel? Then shall I
Not fail to sing His lasting praise on high.

You might think that the whole book would be about Christian's journey to the narrow gate, but here he reaches it, and we're only in chapter four. The point of the rest of the book is, even after entering the narrow gate (also known as "The King's Highway") the road for Christian is difficult and rife with troubles.

At last there came to the gate a solemn person named Goodwill, who asked who was there, where he came from, and what he would like to have.

Goodwill is the keeper of this narrow gate of salvation. In Bunyan's sequel to this story about Christiana, we find out that Goodwill is none other than Jesus Christ himself.

Christian said, "Here is a poor burdened sinner. I come from the City of Destruction, but I'm going to Mount Zion so that I may be delivered from the wrath that is to come. Since I've been told that the way to Mount Zion is through this gate, I want to know, sir, if you're willing to let me in."

"I'm willing with all my heart," replied Goodwill. And with that, he opened the gate.

When Christian was stepping in, the other man gave him a quick pull.

"What does that mean?" asked Christian.

"A little distance from this gate there's a mighty castle of which Beelzebub is the captain," said Goodwill. "From there, both he and those who are with him shoot arrows at those who come up to this gate, hoping they'll die before they can enter."

Beelzebub is a chief demon, and he shoots arrows at all who try to enter the narrow gate. The word literally means "the lord of the flies," and it is also connected with the god Ba'al, worshiped by Israel's Philistine enemies in the Old Testament. We'll see him again as the ruler of Vanity Fair.

"I rejoice and tremble," said Christian.

When Christian was safely in, the man of the gate asked him who had directed him to the gate.

He answered, "Evangelist directed me to come here and knock, as I did. And he said that you, sir, would tell me what I must do."

"See, I have placed before you an open door that no one can shut (Revelation 3:8)," said Goodwill.

"Now I'm beginning to reap the benefit of my dangers!" exclaimed Christian.

"But how is it that you came alone?"

"Because none of my neighbors saw their danger as I saw mine."

"Did any of them know of your coming?"

"Yes," said Christian, "my wife and children saw me at first, and called after me to turn around. There were also some of my neighbors, who called after me to return, but I put my fingers in my ears, and so I came on my way."

"But didn't one of them follow you, to persuade you to go back?" asked Goodwill.

"Yes," he answered, "both Obstinate and Pliable. But when they saw that they couldn't prevail, Obstinate went back shouting abusive words, and Pliable came with me a little way."

"But why didn't he come to the gate?"

"We both came together," said Christian, "until we came to the Slough of Despond, where we both fell. My neighbor, Pliable, got discouraged then and wouldn't venture any farther. He got out of the slough on the side nearest his home and told me that I should possess the brave country alone for him. He went his way and I went mine—he went after Obstinate, and I came to this gate."

"Alas, poor man!" sighed Goodwill. "Is the celestial glory of so little value that he doesn't count it worth the danger of a few difficulties to obtain it?"

Replied Christian, "Truly, I have spoken the truth about Pliable, and if I also go on to say the truth about myself, it will be plain that there's no difference between us. It's true, he went back to his own house, but I also turned aside to go into the way of death, having been persuaded that way by the appealing argument of a person named Mr. Worldly Wiseman."

"Oh, did he land on you?" exclaimed Goodwill. "He would have you seek relief at the hands of Mr. Legality! They're both cheats. But did you take his advice?"

"Yes, as far as I dared," said Christian. "I went to find Mr. Legality, until I thought that the mountain that stands by his house would fall on my head, and I was forced to stop."

"That mountain has been the death of many and will be the death of many more." Goodwill shook his head. "It's good that you escaped being dashed in pieces by it."

"Truly, I don't know what would have become of me if Evangelist hadn't happily met me again as I was absorbed in my thoughts in the midst of my gloomy state. But it was God's mercy that he came to me again, for otherwise I would never have arrived here. But now, here I am, such as I am—more fit indeed for death by that mountain than to be standing talking with you. But oh, what a favor this is to me that I'm still allowed entrance here!"

"We make no objections against any," said Goodwill, "notwithstanding all that they did before they arrived. They're never driven away (cf. John 6:37). Therefore, good Christian, come a little way with me, and I'll teach you about the Way you must travel. Look ahead of you. Do you see this narrow Way? That's the Way you must go. It was built up by the patriarchs, prophets, Christ, and His apostles, and it's as straight as a ruler can make it: this is the Way you must go."

 Even before Christians were called "Christians," they were referred to as "followers of The Way." This, in fact, is how the Apostle Paul refers to those he once persecuted but then joined in Acts 22:4.

Christian asked, "But are there no turnings or windings, by which a stranger may lose his way?"

"Yes, there are many ways that abut this one, and they're crooked and wide. But this is the way you may distinguish the right from the wrong: Only the right way is straight and narrow (Matthew 7:13-14)."

Then I saw in my dream that Christian asked him further if he couldn't help him remove the burden that was on his back, for as yet he hadn't gotten rid of it and couldn't get it off by any means without help.

"As to your burden," said Goodwill, "be content to bear it until you come to the place of deliverance, for there it will fall off your back by itself."

Then Christian began to summon up his inner resources and to prepare for his journey. Goodwill told him that before he went very far, he would come to the house of the Interpreter, at whose door he should knock, and Interpreter would show him excellent things.

Then Christian took leave of his friend, and Goodwill again wished him success on his journey.

Chapter Five

At the Interpreter's House

Christian went on till he came to the house of the Interpreter, where he knocked over and over. At last a person came to the door and asked who was there.

"Sir, here is a traveler," Christian responded, "who was told by an acquaintance of the good man of this house to come calling here for his benefit. I would, therefore, like to speak to the master of the house."

So he called for the master of the house, and after a little time he appeared and asked Christian what he would like.

Christian said, "Sir, I'm a man who has come from the City of Destruction, and I'm going to Mount Zion. I was told by the person who stands at the gate at the head of this road that if I came calling here you would show me excellent things that would be helpful to me on my journey."

"Come in," the Interpreter answered. "I'll show you what will be beneficial to you."

It seems that Interpreter is the Holy Spirit, who, along with the Father and the Son make up the Trinity—that's God as a three-in-one. God's Holy Spirit is variously referred to in the Bible as the Comforter, the Counselor, and the Helper, and here Interpreter leads Christian from scene to scene (remember making dioramas in school?—the scenes are like those) and teaches Christian the meaning of each scene.

So the master commanded his helper to light a candle and told Christian to follow him. They went into a private room, where Christian saw the picture of a very serious-looking person hanging against the wall. It had eyes lifted up to heaven, the best books in its hands, the law of truth written on its lips, and the world behind its back. It stood as if it pleaded with humanity, and a crown of gold hung over its head.

"What does this mean?" Christian asked.

"The person whose picture this is, is one of a thousand," answered the Interpreter. "He can say in the words of the apostle, 'Even if you have ten thousand guardians in Christ, you do not have many fathers, for in Christ Jesus I became your father through the gospel . . . (1 Corinthians 4:15).' 'My dear children, with whom I am again in pangs of childbirth until Christ is formed in you (Galatians 4:19).' You see that his eyes are lifted up to heaven, that he has the best of books in his hand, and the law of truth on his lips—this is to show you that his work is to know and unfold hidden things to sinners, just as you also see him standing as if he were pleading with humanity. And you can see the world as though it were cast behind him, and that a crown hangs over his head: This is to show that by treating the things of the present as being of small importance, and despising them for the love he has of his Master's service, he is sure in the world to come to have glory as his reward.

Now, I've shown you this picture first because the person whose picture this is, is the only person whom the Lord of the City to which you are going has authorized to be your guide. He's been authorized to help in all difficult places you may meet with in the Way. So pay careful attention to what I have shown you, and keep well in mind what you've seen, for fear that in your journey you may meet with some who pretend to lead you right, but whose way goes down to death! (Proverbs 14:12)."

Then, taking Christian by the hand, the Interpreter led him into a very large parlor, full of dust as though it was never swept. When they had looked at it for a little while, the Interpreter called for a servant to sweep. As the room was swept, the dust flew about so abundantly that Christian almost choked on it. Then the Interpreter said to a young woman who stood by, "Bring water and sprinkle the room."

When she had done this, the room was swept and cleaned with ease.

"What does this mean?" Christian asked.

The Interpreter answered: "This parlor is the heart of a person who was never sanctified by the sweet grace of the gospel. The dust is their original sin and the inward corruptions that have defiled the whole person. The one who began to sweep at first is the Law, but the one who brought water and sprinkled the room with it is the gospel. Now, you saw that as soon as the servant began to sweep, the dust flew about so much that the room couldn't be made clean, but, instead, you were almost choked with the dust. This is to show you that the Law, by its working, instead of cleansing the heart from sin, actually revives and puts strength into it and increases it in the soul, even as it uncovers sin and forbids it (Romans 7:9). The Law doesn't give power to subdue sin (Romans 5:20).

 Sanctification is one of those big, theological words in the Christian faith. To a Puritan like John Bunyan, it was understood as the final stage in the process of salvation, the stage at which the saved believer developed into a state of holiness. The great Puritan theologian William Ames wrote in 1629, "Sanctification is the real change in man from the sordidness of sin to the purity of God's image." The Interpreter here explains to Christian that, even though someone is a believer, they need cleansing from sin (symbolized by the sprinkling of water) to remove the dust of their old life.

"Again, you saw the young woman sprinkle the room with water, and afterward the room was easily made clean. This is to show you that when the gospel comes in, the sweet and precious influences of it so affect the heart (as you saw the young woman remove the dust by sprinkling the floor with water) that sin is conquered and subdued, and the soul is made clean through the faith of the gospel. Consequently the soul is made fit for the King of Glory to inhabit (Ephesians 5:26)."

I saw then in my dream that the Interpreter took Christian by the hand and led him into a little room where there were two children, each in a chair. The name of the older was Passion, and the name of the other, Patience. Passion seemed to be very discontented, but Patience was very quiet.

 The first diorama that Christian sees is a scene with Patience and Passion. Patience is able to wait for the good things that God promises, but Passion is hungry for immediate gratification.

Then Christian asked, "What is the reason for the unhappiness in Passion?"

Their governess wants him to wait for his best things till the beginning of next year, but he wants all of it now," replied the Interpreter. "Patience, however, is willing to wait."

Then I saw that someone came to Passion and brought him a bag of treasure and poured it down at his feet. He picked it up and was very happy with it, laughing Patience to scorn. But I watched for a while, and saw that he had wasted it all away and had nothing left but rags.

"Explain this matter more fully to me," Christian said.

"These two children," Interpreter continued, "are symbols. Passion is a picture of the people of this world, and Patience is a picture of the world to come. As you can see, Passion wants everything now, this year—that is to say, in this world. So are the people of this world: They must have all their good things now. They can't wait till next year—that is, until the next world—for their portion of good. The proverb, 'A bird in the hand is worth two in the bush,' is of more authority to them than all the divine testimonies of the world to come. But as you saw that Passion quickly squandered everything away and soon had nothing left but rags, so it will be for all such people at the end of this world."

Christian responded, "I see that Patience has the greater wisdom on several accounts: first, because he's waiting for the best things, and also because he'll have the glory and joy of his when the other one has nothing but rags."

"You may add another," the Interpreter continued. "The glory of the next world will never wear out, but that of this world is suddenly gone. Therefore Passion never had so much reason to laugh at Patience as Patience will have to laugh at

Passion. The first must give place to the last, because the last must have his time to come. But the last gives place to nothing, for there is no other to follow him. The one who has his portion first surely must have time to spend it. But the one who has his portion last must have it lastingly. Therefore, it was said to the rich man, 'In your lifetime you received your good things, while Lazarus received bad things, but now he is comforted here and you are in agony (Luke 16:25).'"

"I realize, then," Christian observed, "that it's not best to long for things that exist now, but to wait for things to come."

"You're telling the truth," replied his friend. "'For what is seen is temporary, but what is unseen is eternal (2 Corinthians 4:18).' But even though this is so, since things present and our fleshly appetites are such good neighbors to one another, and because things to come and things we sense with our flesh are such strangers to one another, that's why it's so easy to be like Passion and so hard to be like Patience (Romans 7:15–25)."

Then I saw in my dream that the Interpreter took Christian by the hand and led him into a place where there was a fire burning in a fireplace. Someone standing by it was always throwing water on it to put it out. Yet, in spite of this, the fire continued to burn higher and hotter.

Again Christian asked what the scene meant. Interpreter said, "This fire is the work of grace that's worked in the heart. The one who throws water on it to extinguish it and put it out is the devil. I'll show you why, in spite of his efforts to put the fire out, it burns hotter and higher."

With that, he led him around to the other side of the wall where he saw a man with a vessel of oil in his hand, from which he continually but secretly poured oil into the fire.

"This," the Interpreter continued, "is Christ, who continually, with the oil of His grace, maintains the work already begun in the heart. It's because of this that, in spite of all the Devil can do, the souls of His people continue to be filled with grace (2 Corinthians 12:9). And the fact that the man with the oil stands behind the wall to maintain the fire shows that it's hard for those who are tempted to see how this work of grace is maintained in the soul."

 Oil has a significant role in the Bible and the history of the church. It's used to signify God's blessing, as in the familiar Twenty-third Psalm: "You anoint my head with oil." In other Old Testament books, kings are anointed with oil. In the New Testament book of James, Christians are instructed to anoint with oil those who are sick, and churchgoers have used anointing for healing ever since.

I saw also that the Interpreter took Christian by the hand and led him into a pleasant place where there was a stately palace, beautiful to see. At the sight of this, Christian was extremely delighted.

He also saw on the top of the palace, certain persons walking who were clothed all in gold.

"May we go higher?" he asked.

Then the Interpreter led him up toward the door, where a large group of people was standing, desiring to go on, but not daring to do so. There also sat a person at a little distance from the door, beside a table, with a book and an inkhorn in front of him, to take the names of those who would enter the palace door. Christian also saw that in the doorway stood many men in armor to guard it, soldiers who were resolved to do whatever hurt or mischief they could to anyone who entered the door.

Christian was somewhat confused by this, and as he looked he saw a man with a very determined expression on his face come up to the person who sat by the writing table, saying, "Write my name down, sir." When that was done, the man drew his sword, put a helmet on his head, and rushed toward the door at the armed men, who set upon him with deadly force. But the man, not at all discouraged, began cutting and hacking most fiercely. So after receiving many wounds and giving many wounds to those who tried to keep him out, he cut his way through them all and pressed forward into the palace (Matthew 11:12, Acts 14:22). This being done, there was a pleasant voice heard from those inside, coming from those who walked on the top of the palace, saying:

Come in, come in;
Eternal glory you shall win.

So the man went in, and there he was given to wear the same clothing that they wore. Christian smiled and said, "I think that truly I know the meaning of this."

 Christian's no dummy. He's starting to catch on to the meaning of these dioramas, especially this one that looks like a war movie.

Christian felt he was ready to resume his journey, but Interpreter said, "Stay until I have shown you a little more, and then you may go your way."

Again he led him into a very dark room, where a man sat in an iron cage.

Now, the man seemed very sad, and sat with his eyes looking to the ground, his hands folded together, sighing as if his heart were breaking.

The Interpreter invited Christian to talk with the man. "What are you?" Christian asked.

"I am what I was not once," was the reply.

"What were you once?" he asked.

The man replied, "I was once a fair and flourishing professing Christian, both in my own eyes and in the eyes of others (Luke 8:13). I was once, as I thought, on my way to the Celestial City, and even had joy at the thought that I should get there."

"Well then," Christian said again, "what are you now?"

"I'm a man of despair," he answered. "I'm shut up in it, as in this iron cage. I can't get out! Oh, now I can't!"

With the vignette of the man in the iron cage, John Bunyan is wading into another theological controversy: Can a person lose his faith? He seems to indicate that, yes, one can. However, as a Puritan, Bunyan also believed that all are predestined, so the man in the cage was never, in fact, destined to end up in the Celestial City with God.

"But how did you get into this condition?" Christian persisted.

The man said, "I stopped watching and being sober. I gave in to my lusts. I sinned against the light of the Word and the goodness of God. I've grieved the Spirit, and He's gone. I tempted the devil, and he came to me. I've provoked God to anger and He's left me. I've so hardened my heart that I can't repent."

"For what did you bring yourself into this condition?" Christian asked.

"For the lusts, pleasures, and profits of this world," the man answered. "In the enjoyment of these things, I promised myself much delight, but now every one of those things bites and gnaws me, like a burning worm."

The Interpreter interjected, "Let this man's misery be remembered by you and be an everlasting warning to you."

"Well, this is frightening!" Christian exclaimed. "God help me to watch and be sober and to pray so that I may avoid the cause of this man's misery."

Christian was becoming a little eager to leave, but Interpreter again invited him to wait for one more thing. "Then," he said, "you may go on your way."

So he led Christian into yet another room, where there was a man rising out of bed. As he put his clothes on, he shook and trembled.

Then Christian said, "Why does this man tremble so?"

The Interpreter ordered the man to tell the reason for his trembling to Christian, and this is what he said: "Last night as I was sleeping, I had a dream, and the heavens became extremely black. It thundered and lightninged in the most fearful way, so that it put me in agony. So I looked up and saw the clouds moving at an unusual rate, and I heard a great sound of a trumpet. Then I saw a Man sitting on a cloud, accompanied by the thousands of inhabitants of heaven. They were all in flaming fire, as were the heavens too. Then I heard a great voice saying: 'Arise, you dead, and come to judgment.' And with that, the rocks split, the graves opened, and the dead in them came out. Some of them were extremely glad and looked upward, while others attempted to hide themselves under the mountains.

"Then I saw the Man who was sitting on the cloud open the book and command the world to draw near. Yet there was, because of the flame that issued forth and came before him, a considerable distance between Him and them, as between the judge and the prisoners at the bar (Jude 14-15). I also heard it proclaimed to those who accompanied the Man who sat on the cloud, 'Gather together the weeds, the chaff, and stubble, and cast them into the burning lake' (Matthew 3:12, 13:30). And with that the bottomless pit opened, almost where I stood. Out of its mouth there came a great deal of smoke and coals of fire, with hideous noises. To the same attendants, it was said, 'Gather the wheat into his barns' (Luke 3:17). And with that I saw many caught up and carried away in clouds, but I was left behind (1 Thessalonians 4:16-17).

"I, too, tried to hide, but I couldn't, because the Man who sat on the cloud still kept his eye on me. My sins came to my mind and my conscience accused me on every side (Romans 2:14-15). Just then, I woke up from my sleep."

"But what was it that made you so afraid at this sight?" Christian asked.

"Why, I thought the Day of Judgment had come," the other answered, "and I thought I wasn't ready for it. This was what frightened me most, that the angels gathered up others and left me behind. Then, too, the pit of hell opened its mouth just where I stood; and my conscience, too, was afflicting me. I thought, too, as the Judge was keeping his eye on me, that he showed an expression of indignation."

The Interpreter then put a question to Christian: "Have you considered all these things?"

"Yes," he replied, "and they give me hope and fear."

"Then keep all these things so in your mind that they become like long, pointed animal prods in your side, to urge you forward in the way you must go," the Interpreter said.

 We may find it distasteful that the Interpreter tells Christian that this horrible vision of hell should prod him to follow the Way, but this is not unlike the frightening visions of the Last Judgment that we see in the great artwork of the same era. In fact, Michelangelo had painted the Last Judgment scene in the Sistine Chapel in Rome less than a hundred years earlier.

As Christian began to summon up his inner resources and prepare himself for his journey, the Interpreter spoke again: "May the Comforter be always with you, good Christian, to guide you in the way that leads to the city." So Christian went on his way, saying:

Here have I seen things rare and profitable;
Things pleasant, dreadful; things to make me stable
In what I have begun to take in hand;
Then let me think on them, and understand
Why they were shown to me; and let me be
*   Thankful, O good Interpreter, to thee.*

Chapter Six

Christian Loses His Burden at the Cross

Now, I saw in my dream that the highway up which Christian was to go was fenced on either side with a wall that was called Salvation (Isaiah 26:1). Therefore, the burdened Christian ran up this way, but not without great difficulty, because of the load on his back.

He ran this way till he came to a place that was somewhat ascending; and on that place stood a cross, and a little below, at the bottom, a tomb.

Jesus of Nazareth was crucified on a cross in about AD 29 on a hill outside of Jerusalem. The Bible refers to this hill as Golgotha (an Aramaic word), the "place of the skull," and Christians also refer to it as Calvary, from the Latin word for "hill." Jesus was buried nearby, in a donated cave-tomb.

So I saw in my dream, that just as Christian came up to the cross, his burden came loose from off his shoulders, fell off his back, and began to tumble down the hill, and so it continued to do till it came to the mouth of the tomb. There it fell in, and I didn't see it any more!

The cross and tomb act as a kind of black hole, sucking the burden of sin from Christian's back, and devouring it!

Then Christian was glad and bright, and said with a joyful heart, "He has given me rest through His sorrow, and life through His death!" He stood still for a while to look and wonder, for it was very surprising to him that the sight of the cross should relieve him of his burden in this manner. And so he looked, and looked again, until the very springs of his eyes sent water running down his cheeks (Zechariah 12:10).

Now, as he stood there, looking and weeping, three Shining Ones came and saluted him, saying, "Peace be to you." The first said, "Your sins are forgiven you" (Mark 2:5). The second Shining One stripped him of his rags, and placed on him a change of clothing (Zechariah 3:4). The third set a mark in his forehead (Ephesians 1:13), and gave him a roll with a seal on it, which he instructed him to guard carefully as he ran and to present it at the Celestial Gate when he arrived. So they went their way.

Christian gave three great leaps for joy and went on his way, singing as he went,

Blessed cross! Blessed grave! Blessed rather be
The Man who there was put to death for me!

In my dream, then, I saw that he went on in this joyful way down the hill. There he saw, a little to one side, three men fast asleep with chains on their heels. The name of one was Simple, of another, Sloth, and of the third, Presumption.

Now we start to meet the characters who are somewhere along the Way, but don't seem to be progressing toward the Celestial City. First are Simple, Sloth, and Presumption, all chained by their complete disregard for the danger they're in.

Christian, then, seeing them in this condition, went to them to see if possibly he might wake them up, and he shouted, "You are like those who sleep on the high seas, lying on top of the rigging; wake up, therefore, and come away (Proverbs 23:34). Be willing, and I will help you get free from your chains!" Also he told them, "If the one who prowls around like a roaring lion comes by, you will certainly become food for his teeth! (1 Peter 5:8)."

With that, they looked at him, and Simple replied, "I see no danger." Sloth said, "Yet a little more sleep." And Presumption added, "Every tub must stand on its own bottom." And so they went to sleep again, and Christian went on his way. Yet he was troubled to think that persons in such danger should have so little regard for the kindness in his offer to help them, both by awakening them, counseling them, and offering to help them get free from their chains.

As he was troubled about this, he saw two persons come tumbling over the wall on the left side of the narrow way. Soon they hurried and caught up with him. The name of one was Formalist, and of the other, Hypocrisy. As they drew up to him, they began conversing together.

"Gentlemen," Christian asked, "where did you come from, and where are you heading?"

Together they replied, "We were born in the land of Vainglory, and we're going for praise to Mount Zion."

"Then why," Christian continued, "did you not come in at the gate that stands at the beginning of the Way? Don't you know that it's written, 'Anyone who does not enter the sheep pen by the gate, but climbs in by some other way, is a thief and a robber (John 10:1)'?"

Formalist and Hypocrisy said that all their countrymen counted it too far around to go to the gate for entrance, and that, therefore, their usual way was to make a shortcut of it, and to climb over the wall as they had done.

 Next we meet Formalist and Hypocrisy, who have skipped the cross and the tomb by climbing over the walls of Salvation to get onto the Way. They've cheated their way in, and the fact that they still wear rags while Christian has bright and shining new clothes betrays their cheating ways.

Christian countered, "But won't it be counted a trespass against the Lord of the City to which we are going, to violate His revealed will in this way?"

Formalist and Hypocrisy told him that, as for that question, he needn't trouble himself. For what they did they had history and precedent to support them, and they could produce, if need be, testimony that could witness it for more than a thousand years.

"But," said Christian, "will it stand up to a trial at law?"

They told him that that custom, since it was of such long standing—more than a thousand years—would doubtless now be admitted as being legal by an impartial judge.

"And besides," they said, "if we get into the Way, what does it matter which way we get in? If we're in, we're in. As we see it, you're the only one we can see in the Way who came in at the gate. We who came tumbling over the wall are also in the Way. So, pray tell, how is your condition better than ours?"

Christian replied, "I walk by the rule of my Master, while you walk by the crude working of your imagination and whim. The Lord of the Way counts you as thieves already; therefore, I suspect you won't be found true persons at the end of the Way. You came in by yourselves without His direction, and you'll go out by yourselves without His mercy."

To this, they didn't give him much answer, and suggested that he look to himself.

I saw then that they went on, each one in his way, without conferring with one another much, except that these two men told Christian that, as to law and ordinances, they had no doubt that they did them as conscientiously as he did. "Therefore," they said, "we don't see how you're any different from us, except by the coat on your back, which was, as we imagine, given you by some of your neighbors to hide the shame of your nakedness."

 Both the road and the hill ahead of Christian are called Difficulty, and they suggest that Jesus' Way is indeed the "Way of the Cross." The other two options, Danger and Destruction, look easier, but when Formalist and Hypocrisy choose them instead of Difficulty, they discover that Danger and Destruction are, quite literally, dead ends.

"You won't be saved by laws and ordinances, since you didn't come in by the door," Christian said (Galatians 2:16). "And as for this coat, it was given me by the Lord of the Place to which I'm going, in order, as you say, to cover my nakedness. And I take it as a token of His kindness to me, for I had nothing but rags before. This is a comfort to me as I travel. Surely, I think, when I get to the gate of the City, the Lord of it will know me for good, since I have His coat on my back, a coat that He gave me freely on the day when He stripped me of my rags. I have, as well, a mark in my forehead, which you may not have noticed, that one of my Lord's most intimate associates placed there the day the burden fell off my shoulders. I tell you, furthermore, that at that time I was given a sealed roll to comfort me by reading as I go in the Way. I was also told to turn it in at the Celestial Gate, to make my entry there certain. I doubt that you have all these things, because you didn't come in at the gate."

They gave him no answer to these things, but looked at each other and laughed. Then, as they all went on, Christian walked ahead of them, sometimes sighing as he went, sometimes with good cheer. And as he went, he often read from the roll that one of the Shining Ones had given him, and he was refreshed by it.

Chapter Seven

The Hill of Difficulty

I saw then that they all went on till they came to the foot of the Hill of Difficulty, at the bottom of which was a spring. In the same place there were also two other ways, besides the one that came straight from the gate; one turned to the left and the other to the right, at the bottom of the hill. But the narrow Way lay right up the hill, and that one going right up the side of the hill is called Difficulty. Christian now went to the spring (Isaiah 49:10), and drank from it to refresh himself, and then began to go up the hill, saying:

> *This hill, though high, I covet to ascend;*
> *The difficulty will not me offend,*
> *For I perceive the Way to life lies here.*
> *Come, pluck up, heart, let's neither faint nor*
> *fear.*
> *Better, though difficult, the right way to go,*
> *Than wrong, though easy, where the end is woe.*

Christian's two companions also came to the foot of the hill. But when they saw that the hill was steep and high, and that there were two other ways to go, and supposing that these two ways might also meet again with the one that Christian was taking, on the other side of the hill, they were resolved to go in those ways. Now the name of the one was Danger, and the name of the other, Destruction. So the one took the way that is called Danger, which led him into a great wood; and the other went directly up the way to Destruction, which led him into a wide field, full of dark mountains, where he stumbled and fell, and never got up again.

Then I looked for Christian, and saw him go up the hill, where I saw that he went from running to walking, and from walking to clambering on his hands and his knees, because of the steepness of the place. About midway to the top of the hill was a pleasant arbor, made by the Lord of the hill for the refreshment of weary travelers. Here Christian, as he arrived, sat down to rest, pulling his roll out of his chest pocket to read for his comfort as he rested. He also began to take a fresh look at the coat that had been given to him as he stood by the cross. Pleasing himself awhile in this manner, he fell into a slumber, and then into a fast sleep, which kept him in that place until it was almost night. In his sleep his roll fell out of his hand. But as he slept, a person came to him and woke him up, saying, "Go to the ant, you sluggard; consider its ways, and be wise!" (Proverbs 6:6). And with that, Christian suddenly started up, and sped on his way as fast as he could till he came to the top of the hill.

Now when he had reached the top of the hill, he met two persons running at full speed; the name of the one was Timorous, and of the other Mistrust.

"Sirs," Christian said, "what's the matter? You're running the wrong way."

Timorous answered that they were going to the City of Zion, and had gotten up that difficult place. "But," said he, "the farther we go, the more danger we meet with, so we turned around and are going back again."

Timorous (which means "fearful") and Mistrust are running the wrong way, scared by the many dangers that lie ahead of Christian. They try to persuade him to turn back, but he knows that his old life is worse than anything ahead.

"Yes," Mistrust said, "for just ahead of us a couple of lions are lying in the way. Whether they're asleep or awake, we don't know, and we could only think that if we came within their reach, they would quickly tear us to pieces."

Then Christian spoke: "You're making me afraid, but where will I run to be safe? If I go back to my own country, which is destined for fire and brimstone, I'll certainly perish there. If I can get to the Celestial City, I'm sure to be in safety there. I must proceed despite the possible danger! To go back is nothing but death; to go forward is fear of death, and life everlasting beyond it. I'm still going forward!"

So Mistrust and Timorous ran down the hill, and Christian went on his way. But thinking again of what he heard from these men, he felt in his chest pocket for his roll, and it was nowhere to be found. Then Christian was in great distress, for he was missing the thing that used to give him relief and that was to have been his pass into the Celestial City. Therefore he began to be greatly perplexed, and didn't know what to do. At last he remembered that he had slept in the arbor on the side of the hill, and falling down on his knees, he asked God's forgiveness for his foolish act. Then he went back to look for his roll.

But all the way back, who can sufficiently set forth the sorrow of Christian's heart? Sometimes he sighed, sometimes he wept, and often he scolded himself for being so foolish as to fall asleep in that place that was erected only for a little refreshment from his weariness. So, therefore, he went back, looking carefully on this side and that, all the way as he went, if by some happy circumstance he might find his roll that had been his comfort so many times on his journey. He went back in this manner till he came again within sight of the arbor where he had sat and slept. But that sight renewed his sorrow all the more, by bringing freshly to his mind his evil of sleeping (Revelation 2:5). So, therefore, he now went on expressing sorrow for his sinful sleep, saying, "What a wretched person I am! that I should sleep in the daytime! that I should sleep in the midst of difficulty! that I should so indulge the flesh as to use that rest for easing my flesh, whereas the Lord of the hill has erected it only for relieving the spirits of pilgrims!

"How many steps have I taken in vain! This is what happened to Israel: For their sin they were sent back again by the way of the Red Sea, and I'm obliged to tread with sorrow these steps that I might have trodden with delight, if it hadn't been for this sinful sleep. How far might I have been on my way by this time! I'm obliged to tread those steps three times, whereas I needed to have trodden them only once. Yes, and now I'm likely to be kept overnight, for the day is almost over. Oh, if only I hadn't slept!"

By this time he had come back to the arbor again, and there for a while he sat down and cried. But, at last, looking sorrowfully down under the seat, he caught sight of his roll! With trembling and haste, he grabbed it up and put it in his chest pocket. But who can tell how joyful this man was when he had gotten his roll again! For this roll was the assurance of his life and acceptance at the desired place of refuge. Therefore he placed it in his chest pocket, close to his heart, gave thanks to God for directing his eye to the place where it was lying, and with joy and tears committed himself again to his journey. But oh, how nimbly now did he go up the rest of the hill! Yet before he got up, the sun went down on Christian, and this made him again bring the fool- ishness of his sleeping to his remembrance. He began to sympathize with himself: "Sinful sleep, for your sake I'm likely to be overtaken by darkness on my journey! I must walk without the sun; darkness must cover the path of my feet; and I must hear the noise of the frightful creatures because of my sinful sleep (1 Thessalonians 5:6)." Now again he remembered the story that Mistrust and Timorous had told him, how the sight of the lions frightened them. Christian said to himself, "These beasts roam at night for their prey, and if they should meet me in the dark, how can I avoid them? How can I escape being torn to pieces?"

 Honestly, I think Christian's being a little hard on himself here! I mean, his scroll (Bible) fell out of his pocket when he took a nap. I think that's forgivable, and it's also common. I forget things all the time—and, I guess I'm pretty hard on myself, too.

So he went on his way.

Chapter Eight

The House Beautiful

While Christian was lamenting his unhappy failure, he lifted up his eyes and saw ahead of him a very stately palace, the name of which was Beautiful, and it stood just by the side of the highway.

So he hurried forward to see if he might find lodging there. Before he had gone far, he entered into a very narrow passage that was about two hundred yards from the Porter's lodge. Looking very closely before him as he went, Christian caught sight of two lions in the way.

"Now," he thought, "I see the dangers that drove Mistrust and Timorous back." The lions were chained, but he couldn't see the chains. Then he was afraid, and even thought about going back after Timorous and Mistrust, for he was afraid that nothing but death lay before him. But the Porter of the lodge, whose name is Watchful, seeing that Christian made a halt as if he was about to go back, shouted to him, saying, "Is your strength so small? Don't be afraid of the lions, for they're chained, and are placed there to test faith, to show where it is, and to reveal those who have none. Stay in the middle of the path, and no harm will come to you."

Then I saw that he went on, trembling for fear of the lions, but taking good care to follow the directions of the Porter; he heard them roar, but they did him no harm. Then he clapped his hands and went on till he came and stood before the gate where the Porter was.

Christian said to the Porter, "Sir, what house is this, and may I sleep here tonight?"

The Porter answered, "This house was built by the Lord of the hill, and he built it for the relief and security of pilgrims." The Porter then asked where he was coming from and where he was going.

 On every pilgrimage, there are rest stops, and House Beautiful is one of them on Christian's journey. From the top of Difficulty Hill he can see the Delectable Mountains, and he can get the rest that he so badly needs.

"I've come from the City of Destruction, and I'm going to Mount Zion; but because the sun has now set, I would like, if I may, to spend the night here."

"What is your name?"

"My name is now Christian, but my name at first was Graceless."

"But how does it happen that you're coming so late? The sun has set," asked the Porter.

"I would have been here sooner, except that, wretched man that I am, I fell asleep in the arbor that stands on the hillside," Christian replied. "No, even so, I would have been here much sooner if in my sleep I hadn't lost my evidence, and came without it to the top of the hill; then feeling for it, and not finding it, I was forced with sorrow of heart to go back to the place where I'd slept, and there I found it; and now I'm here."

"Well, I'll call out one of the young women of this place, who, if she likes your talk, will take you into the rest of the family according to the rules of the house." So Watchful, the Porter, rang a bell, and at the sound of it, there came out at the door of the house a solemn and beautiful young woman named Discretion, who asked why she had been called.

The Porter answered, "This man is on a journey from the City of Destruction to Mount Zion, but being weary and overtaken by darkness, has asked if he might spend the night here. I told him that after you have talked with him, you may do as seems good to you, according to the law of the house." The young woman then asked Christian where he had come from and where he was going, and he told her. Then she asked him what he had seen and met with in the Way, and he told her. And last, she asked his name.

"It is Christian," he said, "and I have so much the more a desire to spend the night here, because by what I can see, this place was built by the Lord of the hill for the relief and security of pilgrims."

Having been ushered past the lions by Watchman, Christian is introduced to Discretion, Prudence, Piety, and Charity. These four, a cross between ancient Greek Muses and Christian virtues, sit and listen as the pilgrim tells the story of how he got from the City of Destruction to House Beautiful. They then tell Christian many things about the Lord.

So she smiled, but tears stood in her eyes; and after a little pause, she said, "I'll call two or three more of the family." So she ran to the door, and called out Prudence, Piety, and Charity, who, after a little more conversation with him, welcomed him into the family. Many of them, meeting him at the threshold of the house, said, "Come in, blessed of the Lord; this house was built by the Lord of the hill for the purpose of entertaining pilgrims such as you." Bowing his head, he followed them into the house. When he was inside, they gave him something to drink, and agreed together that until supper was ready, some of them should have some conversation with Christian, for the best use of the time. And they appointed Piety, Prudence, and Charity to converse with him.

Piety began: "Come, good Christian, since we've been so loving to you to receive you into our house this night, let us, if perhaps we might be able to better ourselves, talk with you of the things that have happened to you in your pilgrimage."

"With a very good will, and I'm glad that you're so well inclined," he answered.

"What moved you at first to commit yourself to a pilgrim's life?" Piety asked.

"I was driven out of my native country by a sound that came into my ears," Christian said. "It was the word that if I stayed in that place where I was, certain destruction awaited me."

"But how did it happen that you came out of your country this way?" she asked.

"It was as God would have it," was his reply. "When I was under the fears of destruction, I didn't know where to go. By chance, a person came to me as I was trembling and weeping. His name was Evangelist, and he directed me to the narrow gate; otherwise I would never have found it. It was he who set me on the Way that has led me directly to this house."

"But," Piety continued, "didn't you come by the house of the Interpreter?"

"Yes, and I saw such things that I will remember as long as I live, especially three things: first, how Christ, in spite of Satan, maintains his work of grace in the heart; second, how a man there had sinned himself quite out of hopes of God's mercy; and also the dream of a man there who thought in his sleep that the Day of Judgment had come."

"Why, did you hear him tell his dream?" Piety asked.

"Yes, and a dreadful one it was! I thought it made my heart ache as he was telling about it. Yet I'm glad I heard it."

"Was that all you saw at the house of the Interpreter?"

"No," Christian said. "He took me and showed me a stately palace, and the people in it were dressed in gold. Then there came a bold and daring man cutting his way through the armed men who stood in the door to keep him out, and I saw that he was then invited to come in and win eternal glory. The thought of those things delighted my heart! I would have stayed at that good man's house a year, but I knew that I had further to go."

"What else did you see on the Way?" the young woman asked.

"See!" Christian exclaimed. "Why, I went only a little further and I saw a man, as I thought in my mind, hang bleeding on a tree; and the very sight of him made my burden fall off my back (for I had been groaning under a very heavy burden). This was a strange thing to me, for I had never seen such a thing before. Yes, and while I stood looking up (for I couldn't keep from looking), three Shining Ones came to me. One of them testified that my sins were forgiven; another stripped me of my ragged clothing, and gave me this embroidered coat that you see; and the third set the mark that you see in my forehead, and gave me this sealed roll. And with that, he pulled it out of his chest pocket.

Piety asked another question: "You saw more than this, didn't you?"

"The things that I've told you were the best ones," was Christian's response. "Yet there were some other things I saw. There were three persons, Simple, Sloth, and Presumption, lying asleep a little out of the way as I came along, with iron chains on their feet. But do you think that I could wake them up? I also met Formality and Hypocrisy, who came tumbling in over the wall, in order to go, they claimed, to Zion. They were quickly lost, however, just as I had tried to tell them they would be, but they wouldn't listen or believe. Above all, I found it hard work to get up this hill, and as hard to come by the lions' mouths. Truly, if it hadn't been for that good man, the Porter who stands at the gate, I don't know but that after all I might have gone back again. But now, I thank God that I'm here, and I thank you for receiving me."

Prudence then asked him a few questions and asked him for an answer.

"Don't you think sometimes of the country you came from?" she asked.

"Yes," he replied, "but with shame and loathing. Truly, if I had been attentive to the country that I came from, I might have had an opportunity to return. But now I desire a better country, a heavenly one (Hebrews 11:15-16)."

"Don't you still carry with you some of the things that you were accustomed to associate with?" Prudence asked.

"Yes, but greatly against my will; especially my inward and worldly thoughts, with which all my countrymen, as well as I, were delighted. But now all those things are my grief; and if I could only choose my own things, I would choose never to think of those things anymore. But when I would rather be doing what is best, what is worst is with me (cf. Romans 7)."

 Here Christian confesses that, while his exterior burden was gladly sucked into Christ's tomb, he still carries with him the sinful inner thoughts that are a whole different kind of burden.

"Don't you find it sometimes to be as if you've gotten mastery over those things that at other times trouble you greatly?"

"Yes, but that's seldom; however, those are golden hours to me when such things happen to me," Christian said.

Prudence went on, "Can you remember by what means you find your annoyances to seem as if you had gotten mastery over them?"

"Yes," he answered, "it's when I think of what I saw at the cross—that will do it; and when I look at my embroidered coat, that will do it; also, when I look into the roll that I carry close to my heart, that will do it; and when my thoughts grow warm about the place where I'm going, that will do it."

"And what is it that makes you so eager to go to Mount Zion?" she asked.

"Why, there I hope to see Him alive who hung dead on that cross; and there I hope to be rid of all the things in me that to this day are an annoyance to me. There, they say, there is no death (Revelation 21:4); and there I will live with such company as I like best. For, to tell you the truth, I love Him, because He relieved me from my burden, and I'm weary of my inward sickness. I would like to be where I will never die, with the company of those who will continually cry out, 'Holy, Holy, Holy!'"

Then Charity said to Christian, "Do you have a family? Are you married?"

"I have a wife and four small children," he answered.

"And why didn't you bring them along with you?" she inquired.

Then Christian began crying, and said, "Oh, how willingly would I have done that! But all of them were completely opposed to my going on pilgrimage."

But Charity persisted. "You should have talked to them, and you should have tried to show them the danger of being left behind."

"I did that," he insisted. "I also told them what God had shown me about the destruction of our city. But it seemed to them as if I were mocking, and they didn't believe me (Genesis 19:14)."

"And did you pray to God that He would bless your words of counsel to them?"

"Yes, and I did that with much affection. For you must know that my wife and poor children were very dear to me."

"But did you tell them of your own sorrow, and fear of destruction? For I suppose that this destruction was visible enough to you," Charity said.

"Yes," he replied sadly. "Over and over and over. They could see my fears in my face, in my tears, and in my trembling at the thought of the judgment that hung over our heads. But all this wasn't enough to prevail with them to come with me."

"But what could they say for themselves as to why they didn't come?" she asked.

Christian looked at her sadly again. "My wife was afraid of losing this world, and my children were given over to the foolish delights of youth. And so, whether by one thing or by another, they left me to wander in this manner alone."

"But didn't you, with your vain and empty life, stifle everything you said as you tried to persuade them to come away with you?"

"Indeed, I can't be proud of my life," said Christian. "I'm conscious of many failings in it. I also know that a person by how they live may soon destroy what by argument or persuasion they try hard to give others for their good. Yet this I can say: I was very careful not to make them oppose my going on pilgrimage by any unseemly action on my part. Indeed, for this very thing they would tell me that I was too precise, and that I denied myself of things, for their sakes, in which they saw no evil. No, I think I may say that, if what they saw in me was a hindrance to them, it was my great fear of sinning against God or of doing any wrong to my neighbor."

"Indeed Cain hated his brother," Charity observed, 'because his own works were evil and his brother's righteous' (1 John 3:12); and if your wife and children were offended with you for these things, then they show that they are not to be persuaded or moved by your entreaties for their own good. Therefore you have delivered your soul from their blood (Ezekiel 3:19)."

While this sounds excessively harsh toward Christian's wife and children, remember that John Bunyan wrote a sequel about her journey to the Celestial City. In other words, they're not beyond God's love.

Now I saw in my dream that they sat talking together in this way until supper was ready. So when they had gotten ready, they all sat down to eat. The table was furnished "with fat things, and with wine well refined (Isaiah 25:6)"; and all their talk at the table was about the Lord of the hill, about what He had done and why He did what He did, and why He had built that house. By what they said, I became aware that He had been a great warrior, and had fought with and killed "the one who had the power of death," but not without great danger to Himself, and that made me love Him all the more (Hebrews 2:14-15).

"For, as they said, and as I believe," said Christian, "He did it with the loss of much blood; but what put glory of grace into all He did was that He did it out of pure love of His country."

Besides, some of the household said they had been with Him and had spoken with Him after He died on the cross; and they attested that they heard it from His own lips, that He is such a lover of poor pilgrims that none like Him is to be found from the East to the West.

They gave him, moreover, an instance of what they affirmed: that He had stripped Himself of His glory, that He might do this for the poor; and that they had heard Him say and affirm "that He would not live on the mountain of Zion alone." They said, too, that He had made many pilgrims princes, even though by nature they were born beggars, and their origin had been the ash heap (1 Samuel 2:8).

In this manner they talked on together till late at night; and after they had committed themselves to their Lord for protection, they went to rest: The Pilgrim they assigned to a large upper bedroom with its window opening toward the sunrise, which was named Peace; there he slept till daybreak.

In the morning they all got up, and after some more conversation, they told him that he shouldn't leave till they had shown him the rarities of that place. First, they took him into the study, where they showed him records of the greatest antiquity. In these they pointed out first the lineage of the

Lord of the hill, that He was the son of the Ancient of Days, and that He was begotten before all ages. Here also were more complete records of the acts that He had done, and the names of many hundreds He had taken into His service. Here, too, he saw that He had placed His servants in such dwellings that neither by length of days nor by the decays of nature could they be broken down.

Then they read to him some of the worthy acts that some of His servants had done; such as how they had "conquered kingdoms, administered justice, and gained what was promised; who shut the mouths of lions, quenched the fury of the flames, and escaped the edge of the sword; whose weakness was turned to strength; and who became powerful in battle and routed foreign armies (Hebrews 11:33-34)."

They read again, in another part of the records of the house, where it showed how willing their Lord was to receive into His favor any person, even though they in times past had offered great intentional insults and offenses to His person and His will. Here also were several other histories of many other famous things, that Christian saw— things both ancient and modern, together with prophecies and predictions of things that will have their certain accomplishment, both to the dread and amazement of enemies, and the comfort and cheer of pilgrims.

The next day they took him into the armory. There they showed him all types of equipment that their Lord had provided for pilgrims—sword, shield, helmet, breastplate, belt, and shoes that wouldn't wear out. And in this place there was enough of this to equip as many soldiers for the service of their Lord as there are stars in the heaven (Ephesians 6:11–17).

They also showed him instruments with which some of the Lord's servants had done wonderful things. They showed him Moses' rod (Exodus 4:1–5); the hammer and nail with which Jael slew Sisera (Judges 4:18–22); the pitchers, trumpets and lamps with which Gideon put to flight the armies of Midian (Judges 7:19–22). Then they showed him the ox-goad with which Shamgar killed six hundred men (Judges 3:31), and the jawbone with which Samson did such mighty deeds (Judges 15:15). They showed him, furthermore, the sling and stone with which David killed Goliath the giant (1 Samuel 17:50); and the sword with which their Lord will kill the Man of Sin in the day when He will rise up in battle. Besides these, they showed him many other excellent things with which he was greatly delighted. When this was done, they all went to their rest again.

The following day Christian wanted to move on, but they prevailed on him to stay one more day, because, they said, "If the day is clear, we will show you the Delectable Mountains." They assured him that this view would further add to his comfort, because these mountains were nearer the desired haven than the place where Christian was at present. So he consented and stayed. The next day they took him to the top of the house and invited him to look south. As he did so, he saw at a great distance a most pleasant mountainous country, beautified with woods, vineyards, fruits of all sorts, and with flowers, with springs and fountains, very delectable to behold (Isaiah 33:16-17). He asked the name of the country. They said it was Immanuel's Land; "and it is as available to all," they said, "as this hill is, to and for all the pilgrims. And when you come there from here," they said, "you may see the gate of the Celestial City, as the Shepherds who live there will show you."

Christian was eager to set forward again, and they were willing that he should. "But first," they said, "let's go into the armory again." So they did; and when they came there, they equipped him from head to foot with what had been tested, for fear, perhaps, he should meet with assaults in the Way. After Christian had been fitted with his armor, he walked out with his friends to the gate, and there he asked the Porter if he had seen any pilgrims pass by. The Porter answered, "Yes, I saw one." "Please tell me, did you know him?" he asked.

"I asked him his name, and he told me it was Faithful."

"Oh," Christian said, "I know him. He's from my town, my near neighbor. He comes from the place where I was born. How far ahead do you think he might be?"

"By this time he's below the hill," the Porter replied.

"Well," Christian said, "good Porter, the Lord be with you and add much increase to all your blessings, for the kindness you have shown me."

Then he started out, but Discretion, Piety, Charity, and Prudence wanted to go with him to the foot of the hill. So they accompanied him, reiterating their former talks, till they came to go down the hill. Then Christian said, "As it was difficult coming up, as far as I can see, it is equally dangerous going down."

"Yes," Prudence said, "so it is, for it is a hard matter to go down into the Valley of Humiliation, as you are now, and not to slip on the way."

"That is why," they said, "we came out to accompany you down the hill."

So he began to go down, but very warily; yet in spite of everything, his foot slipped once or twice.

Then I saw in my dream that these good companions, when Christian had reached the bottom of the hill, gave him a loaf of bread, a bottle of wine, and a cluster of raisins; and then he went on his way.

Chapter Nine

The Valley of Humiliation

Now, in this Valley of Humiliation poor Christian underwent great difficulty. For he had gone only a little way before he saw a diabolically evil creature coming over the field to meet him. His name is Apollyon. Christian began to be afraid, and to wonder in his mind whether to go back or to stand his ground. But he considered again that he had no armor for his back; and therefore he thought that to turn his back to this fiend might give him greater advantage and enable him to pierce him easily with his arrows. So he resolved to take the risk and stand his ground. "For," he thought, "if I had no more in my mind than the saving of my life, this would be the best way to stand."

So he went on, and Apollyon met him. Now the monster was hideous to look at. He was clothed with scales, like a fish (and they are his pride); he had wings like a dragon, feet like a bear, and out of his belly came fire and smoke, and his mouth was the mouth of a lion.

Apollyon is Greek for "The Destroyer," and this vile demon shows up in the biblical book of Revelation leading a swarm of locust-demons (Revelation 9:7–11). Here, Apollyon is the lord of the City of Destruction, and he tries to order Christian to return there.

When he had come up to Christian, he looked at him with a scornful and contemptuous expression, and began to question him in this way: "Where do you come from, and where are you going?"

"I have come from the City of Destruction," Christian answered, "which is the place of all evil, and I'm going to the City of Zion."

Apollyon retorted, "By this I see you are one of my subjects, for all that country is mine, and I am the prince and god of it. How is it, then, that you have run away from your king? If I weren't hoping that you may do me more service, I would strike you now, with one blow, to the ground!"

"I was born, indeed, in your dominions," Christian replied, "but your service was hard, and your wages such that no one could live on them, 'for the wages of sin is death (Romans 6:23).' Therefore, when I had come of age, I did as other prudent people do. I looked out to see if perhaps I might improve myself."

"There is no prince who will so lightly lose his subjects," Apollyon replied, "and neither will I as yet lose you. But since you complain of your service and wages, be content to go back, and what our country can afford, I promise I'll give you."

Christian answered: "But I've given myself to another, namely the King of princes; so how can I, with fairness, go back with you now?"

"You've acted according to the old saying, 'Changed a bad for a worse,'" Apollyon replied, attempting to sweet-talk Christian. "But it's ordinary for those who have professed themselves to be His servants, to give Him the slip after a while, and return again to me. Do this yourself, and all will be well."

"But I've given Him my promise, and sworn my allegiance to Him," Christian protested. "How then can I take this back, and not be hanged as a traitor?"

Pretending to be merciful, Apollyon murmured, "You did the same to me, and yet I'm willing to overlook all that, if now you will turn again and go back into my service."

 The dialogue between Christian and Apollyon is reminiscent of Jesus' dialogue with Satan during the temptations of Christ in the wilderness. The evil one fakes sincerity and twists words, while the virtuous one gives straight and biblical answers.

Christian stood his ground. "What I promised you was before I was of age; and besides, I count the Prince under whose banner I now stand as able to clear my guilt; yes, and to pardon what I did in my compliance with you. And besides, you destroying Apollyon! To tell the truth, I like His service, His wages, His servants, His government, His company, and His country better than yours. Therefore, stop trying to persuade me any further. I am His servant and I will follow Him."

"Consider again when you are in a cooler state of mind," the enemy continued, "what you are most likely to meet with in the Way you are going. You know that, for the most part, His servants came to a bad end, because they're transgressors against me and my ways. How many of them have been put to shameful deaths? And besides, you count His service better than mine, when in fact, He never came from the place where He lives to deliver any who served Him out of the hands of their enemies. But as for me, how many times, as the whole world very well knows, have I delivered, either by power or by fraud, those who have faithfully served me, from Him and His, even though they were taken by them. And so I will deliver you."

Christian said, "His restraint at present to deliver them is on purpose to test their love, whether they will hold fast to Him to the end; and as for the bad end you say they come to, that is most glorious in their account. As for present deliverance, they don't much expect it, for they endure for their glory and then they will have it, when their Prince comes in His glory and the glory of the angels."

"You've already been unfaithful in your service to Him; how do you think you're going to receive wages from Him?" Apollyon asked.

"In what way, Apollyon! have I been unfaithful to Him?" Christian asked, somewhat taken aback.

"You fainted when you first started out, when you were almost choked in the Slough of Despond. You attempted wrong ways to be rid of your burden, when you should have stayed till your Prince had taken it off. You sinfully slept and lost your choice thing. You were, also, almost persuaded to go back at the sight of the lions. And when you talk of your journey and what you've heard and seen, you are inwardly desirous of unwarranted pride in all you say and do."

"All this is true," Christian admitted, "and much more that you've left out. But the Prince whom I serve and honor is merciful and ready to forgive; but, besides, these failings possessed me in your country. I've groaned under them, been sorry for them, and have obtained forgiveness from my Prince (1 John 1:7–9)."

Then Apollyon broke out in a terrible rage, saying, "I'm an enemy to this Prince; I hate His person, His laws, and His people! I've come out purposely to withstand you!"

"Apollyon, beware of what you do!" Christian countered. "For I am in the King's highway, the way of holiness! Therefore, take heed to yourself!"

Then Apollyon straddled completely over the whole breadth of the road, and said, "I have no fear in this matter! Prepare yourself to die, for I swear by my infernal den that you will go no further! Here I will spill your soul!"

With that, he threw a flaming dart at Christian's breast; but Christian had a shield in his hand, with which he caught it, and so avoided being damaged by it. Then Christian saw it was time to rouse himself, so he quickly began to move. Apollyon, just as fast, came at him, throwing darts as thick as hail. Notwithstanding all that Christian could do to avoid it, Apollyon wounded him in his head, his hand, and his foot. This made Christian retreat a little, and Apollyon followed his work at full speed. Christian again took courage and resisted as manfully as he could. This grievous combat lasted for more than half a day, till Christian was almost exhausted. For you can realize that Christian, because of his wounds, was growing weaker and weaker.

Apollyon, seeing his opportunity, began to draw up close to Christian, and wrestling with him, gave him a dreadful fall. With that, Christian's sword flew out of his hand. Then said Apollyon, "I have you now!" With that, he had almost pressed him to death, so that Christian began to despair of his life. But, as God would have it, while Apollyon was readying for his final blow, to make a full end of this good man, Christian nimbly stretched out his hand for his sword, caught it and said, "Do not gloat over me, my enemy! Though I have fallen, I will rise" (Micah 7:8). With that he gave him a deadly thrust, which made him fall back as one who had received a deadly wound. Christian, seeing this, charged at him again, saying, "No, in all these things we are more than conquerors through him who loved us" (Romans 8:37). With that, Apollyon spread forth his dragon's wings and sped away, so that for a while Christian didn't see him any longer (James 4:7).

In this fight no one can imagine, unless they had seen and heard it as I did, what yelling and hideous roaring Apollyon made all during the fight. He spoke like a dragon. Nor can one imagine, on the other side, what sighs and groans burst from Christian's heart. I never saw him all the while give as much as one pleasant look, until he perceived that he had wounded Apollyon with his two-edged sword. Then, indeed, he did smile and look upward. But it was the most dreadful sight that ever I saw!

> *A more unequal match can hardly be—*
> *Christian must fight an Angel; but you see,*
> *The valiant man, by handling sword and shield,*
> *Does make him, though a dragon, leave the field.*

When the battle was over, Christian said, "I will here give thanks to the One who delivered me out of the mouth of the lion, to the One who helped me against Apollyon."

Then there came to him a hand with some of the leaves of the tree of life, which Christian took, and applied to the wounds that he had received in the battle, and he was healed immediately. Sitting down in that place, he ate bread and drank from the bottle that had been given him a little while before, and so, being refreshed, he set forth on his journey with his sword drawn in his hand; for he said, "I don't know but that some other enemy may be at hand." But he met with no other encounter from Apollyon all the way through this valley.

Now at the end of this valley was another, called the Valley of the Shadow of Death, and Christian had to go through it, because the way to the Celestial City lay straight through the middle of it. Now this valley is a very solitary place. The prophet Jeremiah describes it like this: "The barren wilderness, . . . a land of deserts and ravines, a land of drought and utter darkness, a land where no one travels and no one lives" (Jeremiah 2:6).

Now here Christian was worse put to it than in his fight with Apollyon, as you will see by what follows.

Chapter Ten

The Valley of the Shadow of Death

I saw then in my dream, that when Christian had reached the borders of the Shadow of Death, two persons met him, children of those who brought up a bad report of the good land, hurrying to go back (Numbers 13:32).

"Where are you going?" Christian asked.

They said, "Back! Back! And we would have you do so, too, if you value either life or peace."

"Why, what's the matter?"

"Matter!" they said. "We were going the same way you're heading, and went as far as we dared. Indeed, we were almost beyond coming back; for if we'd gone a little further, we wouldn't be here to bring the news to you."

"But what have you met with?"

"Why, we were almost in the Valley of the Shadow of Death, but by happy chance we looked ahead of us and saw the danger before we came to it," they answered.

"But what did you see?" Christian said.

"See!" they exclaimed. "Why the Valley itself, which is pitch dark! We also saw hobgoblins, satyrs, and dragons of the pit, and in that Valley we heard a continual howling and yelling, as from people in unutterable misery who sat suffering in iron chains (Psalm 107:10). Over the Valley hang the discouraging clouds of confusion. Death also always spreads his wings over it. In a word, it's dreadful in every way, being utterly without order" (Job 10:22).

 If you thought the Valley of Humiliation was bad, wait till you hear about the Valley of the Shadow of Death. It's got quicksand on one side and a perilous cliff on the other. Christian has got to stay on the narrow path now, or he risks certain death.

"Then," said Christian, "I realize by what you have said that this is my way to the desired haven."

"Have it your way!" they retorted. "We won't choose it for ours!"

So they parted, and Christian went on his way, but still with his sword drawn in his hand, for fear that he should be attacked.

I saw then in my dream that as far as this valley reached, there was on the right hand a very deep ditch. That ditch is the one into which the blind have been led in all ages and have miserably per-ished there (Psalm 69:14-15). Again, on the left hand there was a very dangerous marsh into which, if even a good person falls, they can find no bottom for their foot to stand on. Into that bog

King David once fell, and no doubt would have suffocated in it if the One who is able hadn't snatched him out (Psalm 40:2).

The pathway here was extremely narrow, and because of this, good Christian was all the more put to it; for when he attempted, in the dark, to avoid the ditch on the one hand, he was ready to tip over into the marsh on the other. Also, when he attempted to escape the marsh, without great carefulness he would be ready to fall into the ditch. He went on in this way, and here I heard him sigh bitterly. For, besides the dangers mentioned above, the pathway here was so dark that often when he picked up his foot to go forward, he didn't know where or upon what he would set it next.

In about the middle of this Valley, I realized that the mouth of hell stood close beside the road. "Now," thought Christian, "what should I do?" And every now and then the flame and smoke would come out in such abundance, with sparks and hideous noises (things that had no fear of Christian's sword as Apollyon did beforehand), that Christian was forced to put up his sword and rely on another weapon, called "Prayer Without Ceasing" (Ephesians 6:18). So he shouted in a voice that I could hear, "Lord, I beg you, save my life!" (Psalm 116:4). He went on like this for a great while, but still the flames continued to reach toward him. He also heard mournful voices and things rushing about, so that sometimes he thought he would be torn to pieces or trampled down like mud in the streets. He saw this frightful sight and heard those dreadful noises for several miles together.

Coming to a place where he thought he heard a company of diabolical creatures coming to meet him, he stopped, and began to ponder his best course of action. Sometimes he had half a thought to go back. Then again, he thought he might be halfway through the valley. He remembered also how he had already overcome many a danger, and that the danger of going back might be much more than to go forward. So he resolved to go on. Yet the diabolical creatures seemed to come nearer and nearer, but when they were almost upon him, he cried out with a most vehement voice, "I will walk in the strength of the Lord God!" (Psalm 71:12–16). So they backed off and came no further.

One thing I wouldn't fail to mention. I took notice that now poor Christian was so perplexed and uncertain that he didn't know his own voice. This is how I understood it: Just when he had come over to the mouth of the burning pit, one of the wicked ones got behind him, stepped up softly to him, and whispered many terrible blasphemies to him. Poor Christian actually thought these had proceeded from his own mind. This put him into greater conflict than anything that he had met before, namely to think that he would now blaspheme the One whom prior to this he had loved so much. Yet, if he could have helped it, he wouldn't have done it, but he didn't have the discernment either to stop his ears, or to know where these blasphemies came from.

Here's another interesting spiritual proposal from Bunyan: that a demon can actually put thoughts into Christian's head and make Christian think that they're his own.

When Christian had traveled in this dejected condition for a considerable amount of time, he thought he heard the voice of a person as if someone were going before him, saying, "Even though I walk through the darkest valley, I will fear no evil, for you are with me" (Psalm 23:4).

Then he was glad for these reasons:

First, because he gathered from this that others who had reverence for God were in this valley as well as himself.

Second, he realized that God was with them, even though they were in that dark and dismal state. "And why not," he thought, "with me as well? Although, due to the difficulties of this place, I can't see or feel it with my senses."

Third, he hoped, if he could catch up them, to have company after a while.

So he went on, and called to the one whose voice he heard ahead of him, but that one didn't know either how to answer him, not knowing anyone else was on the road. After a while the day broke. Then said Christian, "He turns midnight into dawn" (Amos 5:8).

Now when morning had come, Christian looked back—not out of any desire to return, but to see by the light of day what hazards he had gone through in the dark. He saw more perfectly the ditch that was on the one hand and the marsh that was on the other. He saw, too, how narrow the way was that led between them both, as well as the hobgoblins, satyrs, and dragons of the pit. But they were all far off now, for after the break of day they wouldn't come near him. Yet they were made visible to him according to what is written: "He reveals the deep things of darkness, and brings utter darkness into the light" (Job 12:22).

Christian was very moved by his deliverance from all the dangers of his solitary way. Those dangers, though he had been more afraid of them before, he saw more clearly now because the light of day made them visible to him. About this time the sun was rising, and this was another mercy to Christian. For you must note that though the first part of the Valley of the Shadow of Death was very dangerous, this second part that he was yet to go through, was, if possible, far more dangerous. From the place where he now stood, all the way to the end of the Valley, the Way was set full of traps, devices, and nets here, and so full of pits, pitfalls, deep holes, and slopes down there, that, if it had been as dark now as it had been in the first part of the way, even if he had a thousand souls, they would have, in all probability, been thrown away. But, as I said just now, the sun was rising!

Then he said, "His lamp shone on my head and by his light I walked through darkness" (Job 29:3).

In this light he came to the end of the valley.

Chapter Eleven

Faithful's Testimony

As Christian went on his way, he came to a small hill that had been made so that pilgrims might see out in front of them. Christian went up, and looking forward, saw Faithful ahead of him on his journey. Christian called out loudly, "Hello! Hello! Say! Wait, and I'll travel with you!"

At that Faithful looked behind him, as Christian shouted again, "Wait! Wait till I come up to you!" But Faithful answered, "No, I'm running for my life, and the avenger of blood is behind me."

At this, Christian summoned all his strength and quickly caught up with Faithful, and actually ran beyond him. So the last was first. Christian then smiled out of vain pride, because he had gotten ahead of his brother; but not taking good care where he stepped, he suddenly stumbled and fell, and couldn't get up again until Faithful came up to help him.

Faithful was a neighbor of Christian's back in the City of Destruction. He set out on his journey to the Celestial City after Christian had inspired him.

Then I saw in my dream that they went on together in a very loving manner, and had a pleasant and rewarding conversation about all the things that had happened to them in their pilgrimage.

Christian began, "My honored and well-beloved brother, Faithful, I'm glad that I've caught up to you, and that God has so tempered our spirits that we can walk as companions on this pleasant path."

Faithful replied, "I had thought, dear friend, to have your company beginning at our town. But you got started ahead of me, and so I was forced to come this much of the way alone.

"How long did you stay in the City of Destruction before you set out after me on your pilgrimage?" asked Christian.

"Till I could stay no longer," his friend answered. "For there was great talk after you had left, that our city would, in a short time, be burned down to the ground."

"What? Did your neighbors talk like that?"

"Yes," he replied, "for a while it was in every-body's mouth."

"But did no one other than you come out to escape the danger?" Christian asked.

Faithful shook his head. "Though there was, as I said, a great deal of talk for awhile, I don't think they truly believed it. In the heat of the discourse, for instance, I heard some of them speak mockingly of you and your desperate journey (as they called your pilgrimage), but I did believe and do still that our city will end with fire and brimstone from above, and because of this I made my escape."

"Did you hear any talk of our neighbor Pliable?" Christian said.

"Yes, Christian, I heard that he followed you till he came to the Slough of Despond, where, according to some reports, he fell in. But he wouldn't let it be known that this was the case, though I'm sure of it, because he returned thoroughly covered with that kind of dirt."

"And what did the neighbors say to him?"

Again Faithful shook his head. "He has, since going back, been held in great ridicule among all sorts of people. Some mock and despise him, and hardly anyone will give him any word. He's seven times worse off now than if he had never left the city."

"But why should they be so set against him?" Christian protested, "since they also despise the Way he abandoned?"

Faithful replied, "Oh, they say, hang him, he's a turncoat! He wasn't true to his profession. I think God has stirred up even his enemies to jeer at him and make him a proverb because he abandoned the Way" (Jeremiah 29:18-19).

Christian went on, "Did you never talk with him before you came out?"

"I met him in the streets once," his friend replied, "but he veered away on the other side, as if he were ashamed of what he'd done. So I didn't speak to him."

"Well," Christian said, "when I set out, I had hope for that man. But now I'm afraid he'll perish with the city when it's overthrown. It has happened to him according to the true proverbs, 'The dog returns to its vomit,' and, 'A sow that is washed returns to her wallowing in the mud' (2 Peter 2:22)."

"These are my fears for him, too," Faithful said. "But who can prevent what's going to happen?"

"Well, neighbor Faithful," Christian said, "let's leave him and talk about things that more immediately concern us. Tell me now, what have you met with in the Way as you came? For I know you've met with some things, or else you'll be written up as a great wonder."

"I escaped the Slough that I noticed you fell into," Faithful continued, "and got up to the gate without that danger. But then I met with a woman named Wanton, who almost got me into real trouble."

"It was good that you escaped her net," the other commented. "Joseph was hard put to it by her, and he escaped her as you did, but it almost cost him his life (Genesis 39:11–20). But what did she do to you?"

"You can't believe what a flattering tongue she had," Faithful answered. "She pressed me to turn aside with her, promising me every kind of satisfaction."

"No," Christian observed, "she did not promise you the satisfaction of a good conscience."

"You know what I mean," Faithful replied, "every physical and fleshly satisfaction."

It's a little surprising that we've come this far in the story with no talk of the temptation of sexual lust, but here Christian hears his friend Faithful recount how he almost gave in to the lure of a woman named Wanton.

"Thank God you escaped her! 'The mouth of an adulterous woman is a deep pit; a man who is under the Lord's wrath falls into it' (Proverbs 22:14)."

"No, as a matter of fact, I don't know whether I did completely escape her," Faithful said, shaking his head.

"What? I trust you didn't consent to her desire?" Christian exclaimed.

"No, I didn't defile myself, because I remembered an old writing that I had seen, 'Her steps lead straight to the grave' (Proverbs 5:5). So I shut my eyes, because I was determined not to be bewitched by her looks (Job 31:1). Then she hurled abusive language at me, and I went on my way."

"Did you meet with any other assault as you came?" Christian inquired.

Faithful answered, "When I came to the foot of the hill called Difficulty, I met with a very old man who asked me who I was and where I was headed.

I told him that I'm a pilgrim, going to the Celestial City. Then the old man said, 'You look like an honest fellow. Will you be content to live with me for the wages I'll give you?' I asked his name, and where he lived. He said his name was Adam the First and that he lived in the town of Deceit. I asked him then what was his work and what wages he would give. He told me that his work was many delights and his wages, that I should be his heir at the end. I further asked him what house he kept and what other servants he had. So he told me that his house was maintained with all the dainties in the world, and that his servants were those of his own children. He said that he had three daughters, the Lust of the Flesh, the Lust of the Eyes, and the Pride of Life, and that I should marry them all if I wanted to (1 John 2:16). Then I asked how long he wanted me to live with him. He told me, as long as he lived himself."

"Well, and what conclusion did you and the old man reach at last?" Christian asked.

"Why, at first, I found myself somewhat inclined to go with the man, for I thought he spoke very well. But then I looked at his forehead as I talked with him, and there I saw written, "Put off your old self, which is being corrupted by its deceitful desires" (Ephesians 4:22).

"And what then?"

"Then it came burning hot into my mind, that whatever he said and however he flattered, when he got me home to his house, he would sell me for a slave! So I told him to stop talking, because I would never come near the door of his house. He assailed me with abusive language then, and told me that he would send one after me who would make my way bitter to my soul. So I turned to go away from him, but just as I turned, I felt him take hold of my flesh and give me such a deadly jerk back that I thought he had pulled part of me after himself. This made me cry out, 'What a wretched man I am!' (Romans 7:24). So I went on my way up the hill.

 Bunyan's anti-Semitism comes out again in this chapter. He disparages two Old Testament figures: first Adam, whom he makes into a deceitful old man, and then Moses, whom he portrays as one who knows only law and nothing of God's mercy.

"Now when I had gotten about halfway up, I looked behind me and saw one coming after me swift as the wind; so he overtook me just about the place where the little wayside refuge stands."

"Right there," Christian said, "I sat down to rest and was overcome with sleep. It was there I lost this roll out of my chest pocket!"

"But, good brother, hear me out!" Faithful exclaimed. "As soon as the man overtook me, he was nothing but a word and fists, because he hit me and nearly beat me to death. But when I had come to myself again, I asked him why he had treated me like that, and he said it was because of my secret inclination to old Adam the First. With that, he struck me another deadly blow to the chest and beat me down backward! I lay as if I were dead at his feet. When I came to myself again, I cried to him for mercy, but he said, 'I don't know how to show mercy!' and with that, he knocked me down again! I don't doubt that he would have made an end of me, except that another came by and told him to stop."

"Who was that who told him to stop?" Christian asked eagerly.

"I didn't know Him at first, but as He went by, I saw the holes in His hands and in His side. Then I concluded that He was our Lord. So I went up the hill."

"That man who overtook you was Moses," Christian asserted. "He spares no one and doesn't know how to show mercy to those who transgress his law."

"I know it very well," the other mused. "It wasn't the first time he had met up with me. He's the one who came to me when I was living securely at home and told me that he would burn my house over my head if I stayed there!"

"But didn't you see the house that stood there on the top of the hill on which Moses met you?" Christian asked.

"Yes," Faithful said, "and I saw the lions, too, before I came to it. But I think the lions were asleep, for it was about noon. And because I had so much of the day before me, I went on down the hill."

"The porter told me that he saw you pass," Christian said. "But I wish you had stopped at the house, for they would have shown you many rare things that you couldn't forget till the day of your death. But do tell me, didn't you meet anybody in the Valley of Humiliation?"

"Yes, I met with a man called Discontent, who would have persuaded me to go back with him if he could," Faithful said. "His reason was that the valley was altogether without honor. He told me, besides, that to go there would offend all my friends—Pride, Arrogance, Self-conceit, Worldly-glory, and others he said he knew, who would be very much offended if I made such a fool of myself as to wade through this valley."

"Well, and how did you answer him?" Christian smiled as he asked the question.

"I told him that although all these whom he named might claim to be kin to me (and rightly so, for indeed they were my relations according to the flesh), yet since I had become a pilgrim, they had disowned me, and I also have rejected them, so they were to me now no more than if they had never been of my lineage.

"I told him furthermore, that as far as this valley was concerned, he had quite misrepresented the whole thing: 'for before honor is humility, and a haughty spirit before a fall' (cf. Proverbs 16:18). Therefore, I said, I would rather go through this valley to the honor that was so accounted by the wisest persons than choose what he thought was most worthy of our affections."

"Did you meet with anything else in that valley?" Christian asked.

"Yes," his friend said, "I met with Shame. Of all the persons that I met with in my pilgrimage, I think he has the wrong name. The others would leave off after a little argument and resistance, but this bold-faced Shame would never give up."

"Why, what did he say to you?"

Why, he objected against religion itself!" Faithful exclaimed. "He said it was a pitiful, low, sneaking business for a person to mind religion. He said that a tender conscience is a cowardly thing, and that for a person to watch over their words and ways so as to refuse the unbridled liberty that the brave spirits of the time enjoy, would make a person the ridicule of the age. He objected also, that only a few of the mighty, rich, or wise are ever of my opinion (1 Corinthians 1:26). And none of them are of my opinion, either, before they're persuaded to be fools and to be so voluntarily stupid as to risk the loss of everything for nobody knows what! He objected, too, to the low and despised estate and condition of those who have been the majority of the pilgrims of the times in which they lived. He went on at great length, rebuking their ignorance and lack of understanding in all the natural sciences.

"Yes, he went on in that manner about a great many more things than I'm telling here, such as, it's a shame to sit whining and mourning under a sermon, and a shame to come sighing and groaning home; that it's a shame to ask one's neighbor forgiveness for petty faults, or to make restitution where I've taken anything from anyone. He said that religion makes people lose their harmonious relationship with the great because of the latter's few vices (which he called by finer names), and that it makes people own and respect despised and lowborn persons simply because they're of the same religious group. And isn't this, he said, a shame?"

"And what did you say to him?" Christian asked.

"Say? I couldn't tell what to say at first!" Faithful said. "He made me blush, and I felt confused and embarrassed. But finally I began to remember that 'what people value highly is detestable in God's sight' (Luke 16:15). I thought again, this Shame tells me what people are, but tells me nothing of what God is, or the Word of God is. Then I thought of Judgment Day, when we won't be given death or life according to the swaggering and bullying spirits of the world, but according to the wisdom and law of the Most High. Therefore, I thought, what God says is best, indeed is best, even though everyone in the world may be against it.

"Seeing then, that God prefers His religion; seeing that God prefers a tender conscience; seeing that those who make themselves fools for the kingdom of heaven are the wisest, and that the poor person who loves Christ is richer than the greatest person in the world who hates Him: Shame, depart! You're an enemy of my salvation! Will I entertain you against my sovereign Lord? If I do that, how will I look Him in the face at His coming? If I'm ashamed of His ways and His servants now, how can I expect the blessing then?" (Mark 8:38).

"But this Shame was a bold villain! I could hardly shake his company. Yes, he kept on haunting me, continually whispering in my ear about one or other of the weaknesses that accompany religion. But at last I told him it was useless for him to try any further in his designs, because those things he despised, in those I see the most glory! And so, at last I got past this persistent one."

Christian smiled at his friend. "I'm glad, brother," he said, "that you withstood this villain so bravely, for, as you say, he has the wrong name. He's so bold as to follow us in the streets and to try to put us to shame before everyone—that is, to make us ashamed of everything that is good. But if he weren't so audacious himself, he would never attempt to do as he does. But let's continue to resist him, because in spite of all his defiant, swaggering behavior, he promotes the fool and no one else. 'The wise inherit honor,' as Solomon said, 'but fools get only shame' (Proverbs 3:35)."

"I think we must cry to Him for help against this Shame," said Faithful, "to the One who would have us to be valiant for the truth on earth."

"Indeed! but didn't you meet anyone else?" Christian still wondered about Apollyon, and whether his friend had encountered him in that dark valley.

"No," said Faithful. "I had sunshine all the way through that valley, and also through the Valley of the Shadow of Death."

"It was good that you did," Christian observed. "You can be sure it was otherwise with me. For a long period, as soon as I entered into that valley, I had a dreadful combat with that diabolical creature Apollyon and thought he was actually going to kill me, especially when he got me down and crushed me under him, as if he wanted to pound me to pieces. As he threw me, my sword flew out of my hand, and he told me he was sure he had me then! But I cried to God, and He heard me and delivered me out of all my troubles (Psalm 54:7).

"Then I entered into the Valley of the Shadow of Death and had no light for almost halfway through it. I thought I would be killed there, over and over; but at last day broke, and the sun rose, and I went through what was left with far more ease and quiet."

Chapter Twelve

Talkative Joins the Pilgrims

I saw in my dream that as they went on, Faithful noticed a person walking at some distance beside them on the road, for in this place there was room enough for all of them to walk. He was a tall man, somewhat more attractive at a distance than close at hand. To this man Faithful spoke in this manner:

"Friend, where are you going? Are you on your way to the heavenly country?"

"Yes," the man replied, "I'm going to the same place."

"Well, then I hope we may have your good company."

"With a very good will I will walk with you," replied the stranger.

"Come on then," Faithful said, "and let's continue on together, and spend our time talking of profitable things."

"It's very acceptable to me to talk of good things with you or with any other," the newcomer said. "I'm glad that I've met up with those who incline to such a good work, because, to be truthful, there are few who care to spend their time in such a way. Most people, I find, would rather spend their time speaking of things that really don't matter, and this bothers me."

"That is indeed a thing to be lamented," Faithful commented. "What things are so worthy of the use of the human tongue and mouth on earth as the things of God in heaven?"

I like you wonderfully well," the newcomer went on. "Your sayings are full of conviction. I'll add, what thing is so pleasant and what so profitable as to talk of the things of God? What things are so pleasant, that is, if a person has any delight in things that are wonderful? For instance, if a person delights to talk of history or the mystery of things, or if a person loves to talk of miracles, wonders, or signs, where will he find things written that are as delightful and sweetly written as in the Holy Scriptures?"

"That is true," Faithful said. "But our aim should be to be benefited by such things in our talk."

"That's what I said," the other retorted. "For to talk of such things is profitable. By so doing, a person may get knowledge of many things, such as the vanity of earthly things and the benefit of things above. Thus, in general, but more particularly, by doing this, a person may learn the necessity of the new birth, the insufficiency of our works, the need of Christ's righteousness, and so on and so on. Besides, by this, a person may learn, by talking, what it is to repent, to pray, to suffer, and the like.

By this also, a person may learn what are the great promises and consolations of the gospel, to their own comfort. Furthermore, by talking, a person may learn to refute false opinions, to vindicate the truth, and to instruct the ignorant!"

Faithful hesitated a little before remarking, "All this is true, and I am glad to hear these things from you."

Talkative hurried on: "Alas! The lack of this is the cause that so few understand the need of faith, and the necessity of a work of grace in their soul in order to attain eternal life. Instead, they ignorantly live in the works of the law, by which no one can by any means obtain the kingdom of heaven."

"But, with your permission," Faithful interjected, "heavenly knowledge of these things is the gift of God. No one can get it by human effort or only by talking of them."

"All this I know very well," the other said, "for no one can receive anything unless it is given them from heaven. Everything comes from grace, not from works. I could give you a hundred scriptures for confirming this!"

"Well then," Faithful said, "what is the one thing that we will at this time base our conversation upon?"

"What you will," Talkative said. "I will talk of things heavenly or things earthly, things moral or things evangelical; things sacred or things profane, things past or things to come, things foreign or things at home, things more essential or things circumstantial—provided that it all is done to our profit."

Now Faithful began to wonder, and stepping to Christian (for he was walking alone all this time), he said to him, softly, "What a good companion we have here! Surely this man will make a very excellent pilgrim."

At this, Christian modestly smiled and said, "This person, with whom you are so taken, will with that tongue of his beguile twenty people who don't know him!"

"Do you know him then?" Faithful asked.

Know him!" Christian exclaimed. "I know him better than he knows himself!"

Who is he, then?" Faithful asked, glancing at Talkative.

His name is Talkative," Christian said. "He lives in our town, and I'm surprised that you don't know him, though I realize that our town is a large one."

Talkative is a funny character—he has a quick wit and a quick tongue, but his faith seems to go no further than words. Christian asserts that Mr. Talkative has neither the changed heart nor the actions to indicate that he is truly full of faith.

"What family does he come from? And where does he live?" Faithful inquired.

He's the son of a man named Say-well; he lived on Prating Row, and he's known to everyone acquainted with him by the name of Talkative of Prating Row. Notwithstanding his fine tongue, he's actually a sorry fellow."

"Well, he seems to be a very clever person," Faithful rejoined.

Christian replied, "Yes, to those who have no thorough knowledge of him. He's best away from home, because near home he's known to be ugly enough. Your saying that he's a clever person brings to my mind what I've observed in the work of a painter whose pictures show best at a distance, but close up are less pleasing!"

"But I almost think you're joking, because you smiled," his friend continued.

"God forbid that I should joke about this matter even though I smiled!" Christian exclaimed. "And God forbid that I should accuse anyone falsely! I will tell you this, too, about him. This person is for any company and for any talk. As he talks now with you, so will he talk when he's drinking in an alehouse; and the more drink he has in his head, the more of those things he has in his mouth. Religion has no place in his heart or home, nor in his manner of life. All he has lies in his tongue, and his religion is to make a noise with it."

"Is that so?" Faithful said emphatically. "Then I'm greatly deceived by this person."

"Deceived? You may be sure of it. Remember the proverb, 'They do not practice what they preach' (Matthew 23:3). But 'the kingdom of God is not a matter of talk but of power' (1 Corinthians 4:20). This person talks of prayer, of repentance, of faith, and of the new birth; but he only knows to talk about them. I've been in his family and have observed him both at home and away, and I know that what I say about him is the truth. His home is as empty of faith in God as the white of an egg is of taste. It contains neither prayer, nor any sign of repentance for sin—yes, the animals, who can't speak, in their own way serve God far better than he does. He's the very stain, reproach, and shame of all religion to all who know him.

"There's hardly a good word to be said about him in all that end of town where he lives. The common people who know him say of him, 'A saint when away, and a devil at home.' His poor family finds it so. He's such a rude and uncouth person, a person who speaks so abusively and so unreasonably to his servants, that they don't know how to do anything for him or how to speak to him. People who have any dealings with him say it's better to deal with an outlaw than with him, for they'll get fairer dealings than from him.

"This Talkative will go beyond what an outlaw would do in order to defraud, beguile, and outwit them. In addition to this, he's bringing up his sons to follow his steps, and if he finds in any of them a foolish timidity (for that is what he terms even the first appearance of a tender conscience), he calls them fools and blockheads, and will not employ them himself, nor recommend them to anyone else. For my part, I'm of the opinion that he has, by his wicked life, caused many to stumble and fall, and will be the ruin of many more, if God doesn't prevent it."

"Well, my brother," Faithful said gravely, "I'm bound to believe you; not only because you say you know him, but because you have always, as a Christian should, spoken only the truth concerning others. I can't think that you speak these things out of any ill will, but because it is just as you say."

"If I hadn't known him any more than you, I might perhaps have thought of him as you did at first," Christian continued. "And if he'd been characterized in this way only by those who are enemies to religion, I would have considered it a slander—a lot that often falls from bad persons' mouths upon good persons' names and professions! But I could prove him to be guilty of all these things, yes, and a great many more equally bad that I know about. And besides, good persons are ashamed of him. They can call him neither brother nor friend! The very mention of his name among them makes them blush if they know him."

"Well," Faithful commented, "I see that saying and doing are two different things, and hereafter I should better observe this distinction!"

"They're two different things, indeed," his friend said. "They're as different as the soul and the body; for as the body without the soul is only a dead carcass, so talking all by itself is only a dead carcass too. The soul of religion is the practical part: 'Religion that God our Father accepts as pure and faultless is this: to look after orphans and widows in their distress and to keep oneself from being polluted by the world' (James 1:27).

Bunyan is again dealing with a paradox of the Christian religion: A person is saved solely by God's grace, but holy works and action matter too. Talkative's hypocrisy leads to this famous line: "The soul of religion is the practical part."

"Talkative isn't aware of this. He thinks that hearing and saying will make a good Christian, and thus he deceives his own soul. Hearing is only as the sowing of the seed. Talking isn't sufficient to prove that fruit is indeed in the heart and life. Let's assure ourselves that at the Day of Judgment people will be judged according to their fruits (Matthew 7:20, 13:18–23). It won't be said to them then, 'Did you believe?' but rather, 'Were you doers, or talkers only?' (cf. James 1:22). And they'll be judged accordingly. The end of the world is compared to our harvest; and you know that harvesters are concerned about nothing but fruit. Not that anything can be accepted that isn't of faith, but I'm saying this to show you how insignificant the profession of Talkative will be in that day."

"That brings to my mind a word of Moses, in which he describes the animal that's considered clean," Faithful said. "A clean animal is one that has a divided hoof and that chews the cud—not one that only has a divided hoof, or only chews the cud. The rabbit chews the cud, but yet is unclean, because it doesn't have a divided hoof. And this truly resembles Talkative. He chews the cud, he seeks knowledge, he chews on the word, but he doesn't have a divided hoof—he doesn't part with the way of sinners. Instead, like the rabbit, he retains the foot of a dog or a bear, and therefore he's unclean" (cf. Leviticus 11:1–6).

Christian said, "You've spoken, as far as I can see, the true gospel sense of those texts. I will add one more thing: Paul calls some people—yes, and those were great talkers, too—'a resounding gong or a clanging cymbal' (1 Corinthians 13:1). That means, as he explains in another place, 'lifeless things that make sounds' (1 Corinthians 14:7). By 'lifeless things,' he's talking about things that lack the true faith and grace of the gospel, and consequently, things that will never be placed in the kingdom of heaven among those who are the children of life. However, by their sound and by their talk, these things appear as though they were from the tongue of an angel!"

"Well, I wasn't so fond of his company at first, but I'm sick of it now," Faithful said emphatically. "But what should we do to get rid of him?"

"Take my advice, and do as I tell you, and you'll find that he'll soon be sick of your company, too, unless God touches his heart and turns it," the other advised.

"What would you have me to do?"

"Why, go to him, and enter into some serious discourse about the power of religion," Christian said. "Ask him plainly, when he has approved of it (for he will do that!), whether or not this thing is set up in his heart, his home, and his way of life."

Then Faithful stepped forward again, and said to Talkative, "Come, what news do you have? How are you now?"

"Thank you, well," Talkative replied. "I thought we would have had a great deal of talk by this time."

"Well, if you like, we'll have it now," Faithful replied. "And since you left it with me to state the question, let it be this: How does the saving grace of God reveal itself, when it's in the human heart?"

"I perceive then that our talk must be about the power of things," Talkative bubbled. "Well, this is a very good question, and I'll be willing to answer you. And take my answer in brief, like this: First, where the grace of God is in the heart, it causes a great outcry there against sin. Second—"

"Wait!" Faithful cried, "hold on! Let's consider one at a time. I think you should rather say, it shows itself by inclining the soul to look on sin with loathing and horror."

Talkative looked puzzled. "Why, what difference is there between crying out against sin, and loathing sin?"

"Oh, a great deal," Faithful continued. "A person might cry out against sin because it's considered a good policy to do so. But they can't look on sin with loathing and horror except by a holy hatred of it. I've heard many ministers cry out against sin in the pulpit, who can still abide it well enough in their heart, in their home, and in their manner of life. Joseph's master's wife cried out with a loud voice, as if she had been very holy; but she would willingly, notwithstanding her crying out, have committed adultery with him (Gen. 39:15). Some people cry out against sin just as a mother cries out against her child in her lap, when she calls it a brat, and then starts hugging and kissing it."

 This conversation between Faithful and Talkative contains some fine theological points, and you may have to read it a couple times to really get the difference between their two positions on the inward change that comes with faith.

"I see that you're setting traps in your talk," Talkative rejoined petulantly.

"No, not I," Faithful answered. "I'm only for setting things right. But what's the second thing by which you would prove a discovery of a work of God's grace in the heart?"

"Great knowledge of gospel mysteries," Talkative answered.

Faithful said, "This sign should have been mentioned first; but first or last, it's also false. For knowledge, great knowledge, may be obtained in the mysteries of the gospel, and yet there is no work of grace in the soul (cf. 1 Corinthians 13). Yes, if a person has all knowledge, they may yet be nothing, and so consequently they're not a child of God. When Christ said, 'Do you know all these things?' and the disciples answered, 'Yes,' he added, 'Now that you know these things, you will be blessed if you do them' (John 13:17). He doesn't lay the blessing in knowing them but in doing them. For there's a knowledge that isn't accompanied by doing: 'The servant who knows the master's will and does not get ready or does not do what the master wants' (Luke 12:47).

"A person may have knowledge like that of an angel, and yet not be a Christian. Therefore, your sign of great knowledge of gospel mysteries isn't a true one. Indeed, to know is a thing that pleases talkers and boasters, but to do is what pleases God. Not that the heart can be good without knowledge; for without that, the heart is nothing. There is, therefore, one kind of knowledge and another kind of knowledge. There's a kind of knowledge that rests on the bare speculation of things. But there's another kind of knowledge that's accompanied by the grace of faith and love, that sets a person to doing the will of God from the heart. The first of these will serve the talker, but without the other, the true Christian isn't content. 'Give me understanding, so that I may keep your law and obey it with all my heart' (Psalm 119:34)."

Talkative responded, "Setting the trap again with your words, I see. This is neither edifying nor profitable."

"Well, if you please, set forth another sign of how this work of grace reveals its presence in a person's heart," Faithful offered.

"Not I," Talkative said, "for I see we're not going to agree."

"Well, if you won't, will you permit me to do it?" Faithful asked.

"You're free to do as you wish," Talkative said sullenly.

Faithful continued: "A work of grace in the soul reveals itself, either to the person who has it, or to those who know that person. To the person who has such a work, this is what it does: It gives them conviction of sin, especially of the defilement of their nature and the sin of unbelief. They know that they will be condemned for their unbelief if they don't find mercy at God's hand by faith in Jesus Christ (Mark 16:16). This sight and sense of things works in them both sorrow and shame for sin. Moreover, they find revealed in Him the Savior of the world, and they see the absolute necessity of closing the transaction, accepting Him as Lord and Savior. They find themselves hungering and thirsting for Him, and find it is to those who hunger and thirst for righteousness that the promise has been made (Matthew 5:6).

"Now, according to the strength or weakness of their faith in their Savior, so is their joy and peace, so is their love for holiness, so are their desires to know Him more and to serve Him in this world. But though I say it's revealed in this way to the person who has a work of grace going on within them, because of their corruptions, their abused reason, and their past experiences, they may indeed misjudge this matter. It's important, therefore, that a person have a very sound judgment before they can dare conclude that this is indeed a work of grace.

"To those who know the person, the work of grace reveals itself in these ways:

"First, by a confession of their faith in Christ, founded on experience (Romans 10:10, Philippians 1:27).

"Second, by a life consistent with that confession. By that I mean a life of holiness, heart-holiness, family-holiness (if they have a family), and by holiness in their manner of living in the world. Inwardly, they loathe their sin and regard it with horror, and themselves because of it, in private. Then they seek to suppress sin in their family, and to promote holiness in the world—not by talk only, as a hypocrite or a talkative person may do, but by a practical subjection, in faith and love, to the power of the Word (Ezekiel 20:43, John 14:15). Now, sir, as to this brief description of the work of grace and how it's revealed, if you have any objection, by all means, speak it. If not, then will you permit me to ask you a second question?"

Talkative said somewhat quietly, "No, my part is not now to object, but to listen. So let me have your second question."

"It's this," Faithful replied. "Do you experience the first part of my description of the work of grace, and do your life and your way of living testify to these things? Or does your religion stand in word or in speech, and not in deed and in truth? If you're inclined to answer me in this, say no more than you know God above will say Amen to; and say nothing but what your conscience can justify you in; 'For it is not those who commend themselves who are approved, but those whom the Lord commends' (2 Corinthians 10:18). Besides, to say I'm a certain way, when my life and all my neighbors tell me that I'm lying, is great wickedness indeed."

Then Talkative began to blush at first, but recovering, he replied, "You come now to experience, to conscience, and God, and you appeal to Him for justification for what you've spoken. This kind of talk I didn't expect, nor am I disposed to give an answer to such questions, because I don't count myself bound to answer you, unless you take upon yourself to be a catechizer, teaching the principles of Christian ethics and dogma using questions and answers. Even then, I may yet refuse to make you my judge! But, may I ask, why you ask me such questions?"

"Catechism" is the education of those new to the Christian faith. Talkative says he will only defer to Faithful if Faithful is an official teacher in the church.

Faithful answered, "Because I saw that you were quick to talk, and because I didn't know whether you had anything but notions and opinions. Besides, to tell you the whole truth, I've heard of you, that you are a person whose religion lies in your talk, and that your way of life gives the lie to these words that you profess with your mouth. They say that other Christians don't welcome you, and that the whole cause of religion suffers because of your ungodly life, that some have already stumbled at your wicked ways, and that more are in danger of being destroyed by them. Your religion, an alehouse, and greed, and uncleanness, and swearing and lying, and keeping vain company (to name a few) all stand together. The proverb is true of you that's said of a prostitute, namely, that she's a shame to all women. So are you a shame to all who profess faith in Christ!"

"Since you're ready to listen to reports and to judge as rashly as you do," Talkative said angrily, "I can only conclude you're some sort of ill-tempered or melancholy person, not fit to be talked with in any serious way. And so, I bid you good-bye."

Then Christian caught up with his brother and said, "I told you how it would happen. Your words and his pleasures couldn't agree; he'd rather leave your company than reform his life. But he's gone, as I said. Let him go—the loss is no one's but his own. He has saved us the trouble of leaving him ourselves, for if he continues to go on as he is (as I suppose he will do), he would have been a blot in our company. The apostle says, 'Have nothing to do with such people' (1 Timothy 6:5)."

"But I'm glad we had this little exchange with him," replied Faithful. "It may happen that he'll think of it again. However, I've dealt plainly with him, and so I'm clear of his blood, if he perishes (Ezekial 33:1–6)."

Christian answered, "You did well to talk as plainly with him as you did. There's too little of this faithful dealing with people nowadays, and that makes our faith stink in the nostrils of many, so that they underestimate its worth. When these talkative fools, whose religion is only in word, who are so morally corrupt and empty in their walk in the world, are even admitted into fellowship with the godly, this is confusing and baffling to the world; it brings a blemish to Christianity, and grief to the sincere. I wish that all Christians would deal with such people as you have: Then their lives would either become more consistent with the faith they say they have, or the company of the faithful would be too hot for them."

Christian's words here still ring true today, when some television preachers and fake faith healers give all Christians a bad name.

They went on talking in this way of what they had seen along their pilgrimage, and so made that part of the Way easy that otherwise would no doubt have been tedious to them. For they were now going through a desert-like place.

Chapter Thirteen

Christian and Faithful at Vanity Fair

When they were almost out of this wilderness, by chance Faithful looked back and saw one coming after them whom they both knew. "Oh!" Faithful said to his brother. "Who is this who's coming?" Christian looked back and said, "It's my good friend Evangelist."

"Yes, and my good friend, too," Faithful said, "for it was he who set me on the way to the gate."

Evangelist soon overtook them, and coming up, greeted them, "Peace be with you, dearly beloved; and peace be to your helpers."

"Welcome, welcome, good Evangelist," Christian said heartily. "The sight of your face brings to my remembrance your former kindness and your unwearied labor for my eternal good."

"And a thousand times, welcome," good Faithful said. "Your company, O sweet Evangelist—how desirable it is to us poor pilgrims!"

Then Evangelist said, "How have you been, my friends, since the time of our last parting? What have you met with, and how have you behaved yourselves?"

Christian and Faithful then told him of all the things that had happened to them in the Way, and how they had arrived where they were and what difficulties they had met.

"I'm glad indeed," Evangelist said, "not that you've met with trials, but that you've been victors. For that's what you've been—victors—in spite of your many weaknesses, because you've continued in this Way to this very day.

"I say that I'm glad of this thing, and glad for my sake as well as yours. I have sowed, and you have reaped. The day is coming when both the one who sowed and the one who reaped will rejoice together—that is, if you hold out. 'At the proper time we will reap a harvest if we do not give up' (Galatians 6:9). The crown is before you, and it will last forever; so 'run in such a way as to get the prize' (1 Corinthians 9:24–27). There are some who set out for this crown, and after they've gone a long way for it, someone else comes in and takes it from them. Therefore 'hold on to what you have, so that no one will take your crown' (Revelation 3:11).

"You are not yet out of gunshot of the devil. 'In your struggle against sin, you have not yet resisted to the point of shedding your blood' (Hebrews 12:4). Let the kingdom be always before you, and believe without wavering concerning things that are invisible. Let nothing that is on this side of the world come get within you; and above all, look well to your own hearts and to their desires, for 'the heart is deceitful above all things and beyond cure' (Jeremiah 17:9). Set out resolutely (Luke 9:51). You have all power in heaven and earth on your side (Matthew 28:18)."

Then Christian thanked him for his encouraging and challenging speech, but told him that they would like him to speak further to them, to help them the rest of the way. They knew well, Christian said, that he was a prophet and could tell them of things that might happen to them and how they might resist and overcome them. Faithful, too, joined in asking Evangelist to speak further.

So Evangelist continued his speech.

"My sons, you have heard, in the words of the truth of the gospel, that you must go through many hardships to enter the kingdom of God (Acts 14:22). Again, that in every city prison and hardships await you (Acts 20:23), and that you can't expect that you should go long on your pilgrimage without them in some way or another. You've already found something of the truth of these testimonies, and more will soon follow.

"For now, you see, you're almost out of this wilderness, and therefore you'll soon come into a town that you'll soon see ahead of you, In that town you'll be harshly beset with enemies, who will strain hard to kill you. Be sure that one or both of you must seal with blood the testimony that you hold. But be faithful unto death, and the King will give you a crown of life (Revelation 2:10). The one who dies there, although his death will be unnatural, and his pain perhaps great, will even so have it better than the other—not only because he'll arrive at the Celestial City sooner, but because he'll escape many miseries that the other will meet with in the rest of his journey. But when you've come to the town and you find fulfilled what I've related, then remember your friend, and be courageous, and commit yourselves to your faithful Creator and continue to do good" (1 Peter 4:19).

I saw then in my dream that when they had gotten out of the wilderness, they soon saw a town before them. The name of the town is Vanity, and in that town there is held a fair, known as Vanity Fair. It's kept all the year long. It's called Vanity Fair because the town where it's kept is lighter than vanity and emptiness; also, because all that's sold or comes from the town is vanity. As is the saying of the wise, "All is vanity and a striving after wind" (Ecclesiastes 1:14 RSV).

 The town that Faithful and Christian are now entering is Vanity, which means having too much faith in one's own abilities. This is a sin in Christianity, because it means that a person trusts one's own abilities instead of God's. In this town, a festival is always in session, Vanity Fair, in which all sorts of vanities are on display.

This fair isn't newly built, but is a thing of ancient standing. I'll show you how it began.

About five thousand years ago, there were pilgrims walking to the Celestial City as Christian and Faithful were presently walking. Beelzebub, Apollyon, and Legion, with their companions, realized that the path that the pilgrims made on their way to the Celestial City lay through this town of Vanity, and so they contrived to set up a fair there. It was a fair in which all sorts of vanity would be sold, and it would last all year long. Therefore at this fair all kinds of things are sold, such as houses, lands, trades, professions, places, honors, preferments, titles, countries, kingdoms, lusts, pleasures, and delights of all sorts—such as prostitutes, wives, husbands, children, masters, servants, lives, blood, bodies, souls, silver, gold, pearls, precious stones, and whatnot.

Furthermore, at this fair there is at all times to be seen juggling, cheats, games, plays, fools, mimics, unprincipled persons, and rogues of every kind. Here can be seen, too (and that for nothing), thefts, murders, adulteries, false swearing, and obscenities of all kinds.

 Bunyan's description of Vanity Fair was popularized a century later, when William Makepeace Thackeray wrote Vanity Fair: A Novel without a Hero, *a satire of the nineteenth-century English middle class. That book has been made into several movies, the most recent of which starred Reese Witherspoon.*

As in other fairs of less importance, there are several rows and streets, under their proper names, where various wares are sold. So here likewise you have the proper places, rows, streets (namely, countries and kingdoms), where the wares of this fair are most easily found. Here is the British Row, the French Row, the Italian Row, the Spanish Row, the German Row, where several sorts of vanities are to be sold.

Now, as I said, the Way to the Celestial City lies just through this town where this fair is kept. A person who wants go to the City without going through this town would indeed need to leave the world (1 Corinthians 5:9-10). The Prince of princes himself, when here, went through this town to His own country, and on a fair day, too. Yes, and I think it was Beelzebub, the chief lord of this fair, who invited Him to buy some of his vanities. He would have made Him lord of the fair if He had only done him reverence as He went through the town (Luke 4:5–7). Because He was such a person of honor, Beelzebub took Him from street to street, and showed Him all the kingdoms of the world in a short time, so that he might, if possible, entice the Blessed One to cheapen himself and buy some of his vanities. But He had no mind to buy any of his merchandise, and therefore left the town without laying out as much as one red cent for any of these vanities.

This fair, therefore, is an ancient thing, of long standing, and a very great fair. Now these

Pilgrims, as I said, had to go through it. Well, so they did; but even as they entered the fair, their presence caused a stir among the people, and the town was in a hubbub about them. Several things caused this. First, the Pilgrims were dressed in a different kind of clothing from the kind that was bought and sold at the fair. The people of the fair, therefore, gazed at them, and some said they were fools, others thought they were crazy, some simply called them outlandish.

Second, the people were offended not only by their clothing, but by their speech as well. Few could understand what they said. The Pilgrims naturally spoke the language of Canaan, but those who kept the fair were persons of this world, so that from one end of the fair to the other, the Pilgrims and the persons of the fair seemed like barbarians each to the other.

Third, what offended the persons of the fair the most was that the Pilgrims took little interest in their goods, and didn't care so much as to look at them. If they were called on to buy, the Pilgrims would put their fingers in their ears, crying, "Turn away my eyes from seeing vanity," and they would look upwards, signifying that their trade and traffic was in heaven (Psalm 119:37, Philippians 3:19-20).

One took the risk mockingly, seeing the way the Pilgrims carried themselves, to say to them, "What will you buy?" They in turn looked very seriously at him and answered, "We buy the truth" (Proverbs 23:23). At that the townsmen took offense and began to make sport of the Pilgrims—some mocking, some taunting, some speaking reproachfully, and some calling upon others to beat them. Finally things came to such a hubbub and stirring in the fair that everything was in disorder.

At this point, the great one at the fair was given word about the Pilgrims' presence and all the confusion. He came down quickly and authorized some of his most trusted friends to take these persons in to be examined, since they were turning the fair upside down. So the men were brought to examination. Their examiners asked them where they came from and what they were doing there in such unusual clothing. The men told them that they were going to their own country, which was the heavenly Jerusalem (Hebrews 11:13–16). They said they had given no occasion to the persons of the town, nor to the merchandisers, to abuse them in this manner or to hinder them on their way, unless it could be that, when one asked them what they would buy, they said they would buy the truth.

But those who were appointed to examine them didn't believe them to be anything but lunatics or madmen, or else the type of person who comes to put everything into confusion in a fair. Therefore they took them and beat them, and smeared them with dirt, and then put them into a cage so that they might be made a spectacle to all the persons of Vanity Fair.

There they lay for some time, and were made the object of sport, malice, or revenge—the great one of the fair still laughing at all that happened to them. But the men were patient, and didn't answer the abusive language with more abusive language. On the other hand, when cursed, they blessed, and gave good words for bad, kindness for injuries done.

Some persons in the fair who were more observant and less prejudiced than their companions, began to stop what they were doing, and to blame the baser sort for their continual abuses to the Pilgrims. But this resulted only in stirring up the anger of the mob against them as well, so that they were counted as bad as the Pilgrims in the cage, and were called confederates and told that they should be sharers in their misfortunes. The others replied that as far as they could see, these Pilgrims were quiet and sober, and intended nobody any harm. They said moreover that there were many who traded in the fair who were more deserving of being put into the cage—yes, even to the point of being put in the stocks—than were these persons who had been so abused. After many words had passed on both sides, they fell to blows among themselves, and did harm to one another.

The two Pilgrims had behaved themselves wisely and soberly during all this, but they were again brought before their examiners and charged as being guilty of the near-riot that had been in the fair. So they beat them pitifully, and hanged iron cuffs and chains on them and led them up and down the fair, as an example and a terror to others, to prevent anyone from speaking on their behalf or joining themselves to them.

Christian and Faithful behaved themselves even more wisely, and received the personal humiliation and shame that was cast upon them with so much meekness and patience, that it won to their side several of the persons in the fair, though these were only a few in comparison with the rest. But this put the other party into an even greater rage, to the point where they concluded that these two persons should be put to death. They threatened that neither the cage nor the irons would do, but that they should die for the abuse they had done, and for deluding the people of the fair.

 The imprisonment of the two friends surely has parallels to Bunyan's imprisonment, during which he wrote The Pilgrim's Progress.

Then they were put back into the cage again until further plans could be made, and this time their feet were put in the stocks as well.

Christian and Faithful called to mind again what they had heard from their faithful friend Evangelist, and were all the more confirmed in their way and in their sufferings by what he told them would happen to them. They comforted each other, remembering that the one whose lot it was to suffer would have the best of it. Therefore each one secretly wished that he might have that treatment. But committing themselves to the all wise disposal of the One who rules all things, with much contentment they remained in the condition in which they found themselves until they should be otherwise disposed of.

At the appointed time, they were brought forth to their trial in order to be condemned. The trial judge's name was Lord Hate-good. Their indictments were the same in substance, though they varied somewhat in form. The contents of their indictment were as follows:

"That they were enemies to and disturbers of their trade; that they had made commotions and divisions in the town, and had won a party to their own most dangerous opinions, in contempt of the law of their prince."

Faithful began to answer that he had only set himself against that which had set itself against the One who is higher than the highest. "And," said he, "as for disturbance, I make none, being myself a person of peace. The parties that were won to us were won by seeing our truth and innocence, and they have only turned from the worse to the better. And as to the king you talk of, since he is Beelzebub, the enemy of our Lord, I defy him and all his angels."

Then the proclamation was made that if anyone had anything to say for their lord the king against the prisoner at the bar, they should forthwith appear and give their evidence. So there came in three witnesses—Envy; Superstition; and Pickthank, also called Talebearer. They were then asked if they knew the prisoner at the bar, and what they had to say for their lord the king against him.

Envy stood forth and spoke this way: "My Lord, I have known this person for a long time, and will attest upon my oath before this honorable bench that he is—"

"Stop!" cried the Judge. "Give him his oath!"

So they swore him in, and he continued, "My Lord, this person, notwithstanding his name that gives a deceptive impression of reliability, is one of the most depraved persons in our country. He has no regard for either prince or people, law or custom, but does all that he can to possess everyone with certain of his disloyal notions, which he in general calls principles of faith and holiness. In particular, I heard him once myself affirm that Christianity and the customs of our town of Vanity were diametrically opposite and couldn't be reconciled. By this saying, my Lord, he at once condemns all our laudable doings and ourselves as well who do them."

 Faithful's trial is reminiscent of several biblical stories: Job's questioning by his wife and friends, Jesus' own trials before Herod and Pilate, and the stoning of Stephen, the first Christian martyr.

Then the Judge said to Envy, "Do you have any more to say?"

"My Lord," he replied, "I could say much more, only I wouldn't want to be tedious to the court. Yet, if need be, when the other gentlemen have given their evidence, rather than leave anything lacking to dispatch this person, I will gladly enlarge my testimony against him." So he was ordered to stand by.

Then they called Superstition, ordered him to look at the prisoner, and asked what he could say for their lord the king against this person. Having been sworn in, he began.

"My Lord, I have no great acquaintance with this person, nor do I desire to have further knowledge of him. However, this I know: that he is a very harmful fellow, from some of the conversation that I had with him the other day in this town. I heard him say as I was talking with him that our religion is nothing and that it's the kind by which a person can by no means please God. Your Lordship knows very well what will follow from such talk as this—that we worship in vain and are yet in our sins, and finally we will be damned. And this is what I have to say against him."

Talebearer was then sworn and commanded to say what he knew on behalf of their lord the king against the prisoner at the bar.

"My Lord, and you gentlemen all," Talebearer began, "this fellow I have known of a long time, and I have heard him speak things that ought not to be spoken. For he has bitterly criticized our noble prince, Beelzebub, and has spoken contemptuously of his honorable friends, Lord Old Man, Lord Carnal Delight, Lord Luxurious, Lord Desire of Vain Glory, old Lord Lechery, Sir Having Greedy, with all the rest of our nobility. And furthermore, this man has said that if all persons were of his mind, not one of these noblemen would be allowed to live any longer in this town. Besides this, he has not been afraid to criticize you, my Lord, who are now appointed to be his judge, calling you an ungodly villain, and many other such abusive terms with which he has spattered most of the fine people of our town."

When this Talebearer had told his tale, the Judge directed his speech to the prisoner at the bar, saying, "You renegade, heretic, and traitor! Have you heard what these honest gentlemen have witnessed against you?"

"May I speak a few words in my own defense?" Faithful asked.

"Scum!" cried the Judge. "You don't deserve to live any longer, and ought to be slain immediately right here! But, so that all persons may see our gentleness toward you, let us hear what you, vile reprobate that you are, have to say!"

Faithful spoke. "I say, then, in answer to what Mr. Envy has said, that I never said anything but this, that any rule or law or custom or people that were flatly against the Word of God are diametrically opposed to Christianity. If I've spoken wrongly in this, convince me of my error, and I'm ready here before you to withdraw what I said.

"Second, as to Mr. Superstition's charge against me, I said only this, that in the worship of God there is required a divine faith; but there can be no divine faith without a divine revelation of the will of God. Therefore, whatever is thrust into the worship of God that isn't agreeable to divine revelation can't be done by anything other than by a human faith, which will not be profitable to eternal life.

"As to what Mr. Talebearer said, I say (avoiding terms such as that I am said to speak abusively, and the like) that the prince of this town, with all the rabble, and his attendants whom this gentleman named, are more fit for living in hell than in this town and country. And so, the Lord have mercy upon me!"

The Judge then called the jury, who all this while stood by to hear and to observe.

"Gentlemen of the jury," he said, "you see this person about whom so great an uproar has been made in this town. You have also heard his reply and confession. It lies now in your hearts to hang him or save his life; but yet I think it proper to instruct you in our law.

"There was an act made in the days of Pharaoh the Great, servant to our prince, that, for fear that those of a contrary religion should multiply and grow too strong for him, their males should be thrown into the river (cf. Exodus 1). There was also an act made in the days of Nebuchadnezzar the Great, another of his servants, that whoever would not fall down and worship his golden image should be cast into a fiery furnace (cf. Daniel 3). There was also an act made in the days of Darius, that whoever, for a time, called upon any god but him, should be thrown into the lions' den (cf. Daniel 6). Now the substance of these laws this rebel has broken, not only in thought (which can't be allowed) but also in word and deed. This is absolutely intolerable!

"For the law of Pharaoh was made upon a supposition that it would prevent mischief, since no crime was yet apparent. But here is a crime apparent. For the second and third, you see he disputes against our religion. For the treason he has confessed, he deserves to die."

Then the jury went out. Their names were Mr. Blind-man, Mr. No-good, Mr. Malice, Mr. Love-lust, Mr. Live-loose, Mr. Heady, Mr. High-mind, Mr. Enmity, Mr. Liar, Mr. Cruelty, Mr. Hate-light, and Mr. Implacable. Every one of them handed in his private verdict against him among themselves, and afterwards they unanimously concluded to bring in a verdict of guilty before the Judge. First, among themselves, Mr. Blind-man, the foreman, said, "I see clearly that this person is a heretic."

Then Mr. No-good said, "Away with such a fellow from the earth." "Indeed," Mr. Malice said, "for I hate the very looks of him." Then Mr. Love-lust said, "I could never endure him." "Nor

I," Mr. Live-loose said, "for he would always be condemning my way." "Hang him, hang him," Mr. Heady said. "A sorry, worthless fellow," Mr. High-mind said. "My heart rises against him," Mr. Enmity said. "He's a scoundrel," Mr. Liar said. "Hanging is too good for him," Mr. Cruelty said. "Let's dispatch him out of the way," Mr. Hate-light said. Then Mr. Implacable said, "For all the world I could never be reconciled to him. Therefore let's declare him guilty of death."

And so they did. Presently he was condemned to be taken from the place where he was, back to the place from which he came, and there to be put to the most cruel death that could be invented.

They brought him out to do with him according to their law. First, they whipped him, then they beat him, then they lanced his flesh with knives. After that, they stoned him with stones, pricked him with swords, and last of all, they burned him to ashes at the stake. So Faithful came to his end.

Now I saw that there stood behind the multitude a chariot and a couple of horses, waiting for Faithful. As soon as his adversaries had made an end of him, he was taken up into the chariot and immediately was carried up through the clouds, with the sound of the trumpet, by the nearest way leading to the Celestial Gate.

 The Old Testament prophet, Elijah, was also escorted to heaven in a chariot (2 Kings 2:11).

But as for Christian, he had some respite and was sent back to prison. There he remained for some time, but the One who overrules all things, having even the power of their rage in His own hand, so brought it about, that Christian for all that time escaped them and went his way, singing as he went—

Well, Faithful, you have faithfully professed
Unto your Lord, with whom you will be blessed.
Sing, Faithful, sing, and let your name survive;
For though they killed you, you are still alive.

Chapter Fourteen

Encounter with By-ends and Friends

Christian didn't leave the town alone, but was joined by one whose name was Hopeful, who had been made so by seeing Christian and Faithful in their words and behavior in their sufferings at the fair. This man joined himself to Christian, and, entering a brotherly covenant, told him that he would be his companion. So one died to bear testimony to the truth, and another rose out of his ashes to be a companion with Christian in his pilgrimage. This Hopeful also told Christian that there were many more of the persons in the Fair who would take their time and follow afterward.

Here we see a bit of a loophole: Earlier we were told that the only way to the Celestial City was through the Narrow Gate and under the Cross, but Hopeful, a resident of Vanity Fair, is inspired by Christian's witness and Faithful's martyrdom, and he converts and joins Christian on his journey. Biblically, "faith" and "hope" are linked in 1 Corinthians with "love" as the three great virtues of Christian faith.

So I saw that soon after they had gotten out of the Fair, they overtook a person going before them, whose name was Follow-fairwinds, but who was commonly called By-ends. So they said to him, "Where are you from, Sir? And how far are you going in this way?" He told them that he came from the town of Fairspeech and that he was going to the Celestial City. But he didn't tell them his name.

"By-ends" refers to someone who has a secret interest in something. For Mr. By-ends, he's involved with religion so that he can make some money off it.

"From Fairspeech!" Christian said. "Are there any good people who live there?"

"Yes," By-ends said, "I hope so."

"Tell me, Sir, what may I call you?" Christian said.

"I'm a stranger to you and you to me," the other replied. "If you're going this way, I'll be glad of your company. If not, I must be content."

"This town of Fairspeech," Christian said, "I've heard of it. As I remember, they say it's a wealthy place."

"Yes, I'll assure you that it is," By-ends said, "and I have very many rich relatives there."

"Tell me, who are your relatives there, if I may be so bold?" Christian asked

"Almost the whole town," By-ends said. "in particular, Lord Turnabout, Lord Timeserver,

Lord Fair-speech, from whose ancestors that town first took its name. Also, Mr. Smoothman, Mr. Facing-both-ways, Mr. Anything, and the parson of our parish, Mr. Two-tongues, was my mother's own brother by her father's side. To tell you the truth, I have become a gentleman of good quality, yet my great-grandfather was only a ferryman, looking one way and rowing another. I got most of my estate by the same occupation."

"Are you married?" Christian asked.

Yes," By-ends answered, "and my wife is a very virtuous woman. She was Lady Feigning's daughter, and therefore comes from an honorable family. She comes from such a breeding that she knows how to carry it to all, even to prince and peasant. It is true we somewhat differ in religion from those of the stricter sort, yet in just two small points. First, we never strive against the wind and tide; second, we're always most zealous when Religion goes about in silver slippers. We love much to walk with him in the street if the sun shines and the people applaud him."

Christian stepped a little aside and said to his companion, Hopeful, "It comes to my mind that this is By-ends of Fair-speech. If it is he, we have as true a man of humble birth in our company as lives in these parts."

Hopeful said, "Ask him. I think he shouldn't be ashamed of his name."

So Christian caught up with him again and said, "Sir, you talk as if you knew something more than everyone else does. And if I don't miss the mark, I think I half guess your name. Aren't you Mr. By-ends of Fairspeech?"

"This isn't my name," the other answered. "It's indeed a nickname that's been given me by some who can't stand me, and I must be content to bear it as a reproach, as other good persons have borne theirs before me."

"But did you never give an occasion to anyone to call you by this name?" Christian asked.

"Never, never!" he replied. "The worst thing that I ever did to give them any occasion to call me this name was that I always had the luck to jump in my judgment with the present way of the times, whatever it was. It was my good luck to get good things in this way. But if things fall my way like that, let me count them a blessing, but don't let the malicious sort of person heap reproach on me because of it."

"I thought indeed that you were the person I'd heard of," Christian went on. "And to tell you what I think, I'm afraid this name belongs to you more properly than you're willing to think it does."

By-ends answered, "Well! If you choose to think this, I can't help it. You'll find me to be fair company if you'll still have me as your associate."

Christian answered, "If you want to go with us, you must go against wind and tide, and I gather this is against your opinion. You must also own your faith when it's in rags as well as when it's in silver slippers, and stand by it, too, when bound in irons, as well as when it walks the streets with applause."

By-ends answered quickly, "You mustn't impose, nor lord it over my faith. Leave me to my liberty, and let me go with you."

"Not one step further, unless you will do in this matter as we're prepared to do."

Then By-ends said, "I'll never desert my old principles, since they're harmless and profitable. If I may not go with you, I must do as I did before you caught up to me—go by myself until some person catches up to me who will be glad of my company."

Now I saw in my dream that Christian and Hopeful abandoned him altogether and kept their distance in front of him. But one of them, looking back, saw three persons following Mr. By-ends, and, as they came up to him, he made them a very low bow, which they in turn returned to him. Their names were Mr. Hold-the-world, Mr. Money-love, and Mr. Save-all, persons that Mr. By-ends had been formerly acquainted with as schoolchildren together. In school they had all studied under Mr. Gripe-man, a schoolmaster in Lovegain, which is a market town in the county of Coveting, in the North. This schoolmaster taught them the art of getting, either by means of violence, flattery, lying, or by putting on a disguise of religion. And these four persons had attained much of the art of their master, so that each of them could have kept such a school themselves.

Well, when they had, as I said, greeted each other in this manner, Mr. Money-love said to Mr. By-ends, "Who are those persons on the road in front of us?" (For Christian and Hopeful were still in view.)

"They are a couple of persons from a far country," By-ends answered. "They, according to their own way of doing things, are going on pilgrimage."

"What a shame! Why didn't they stay, so that we might have had their good company?" Money-love asked. "For they, and we, and you, sir, I hope, are all going on a pilgrimage."

"We're indeed doing that," By-ends said. "But these persons are so rigid and love their own notions so much, and have so little regard for the opinions of others that, even though a person might be ever so godly, if the person doesn't agree with them in everything, they push them forcefully out of their company."

"That's bad," Save-all said, "but we read of some that are altogether too righteous. Such a person's rigidness prevails with them to judge and condemn everyone but themselves. But, pray tell, what and how many were the things in which you differed from them?"

By-ends said, "Why, they, after their headstrong manner, conclude that it's their duty to rush on their journey in all kinds of weather, and I'm for waiting for wind and tide. They're for risking everything for God at once; and I'm for taking all advantages to secure my life and property. They're for holding their notions, even though everyone else is against them, but I'm for religion in whatever, and as far as, the times, and my safety, will bear it. They're for Religion when it's clothed in rags and held in contempt, but I'm for Mr. Religion when he walks in his golden slippers in the sunshine and with applause."

Mr. Hold-the-world spoke: "Yes, indeed, good Mr. By-ends. Because, for my part, I can only count a person to be a fool if, having the liberty to keep what they have, they should be so unwise as to lose it. Let's be wise as serpents; it's best to make hay when the sun shines. You see how the bee lies still all winter, and stirs itself only when it can have profit with pleasure. God sometimes sends rain and sometimes sun. If they're such fools as to go through the first, let us yet be content to take fair weather along with us. For my part, I like the religion best that will stand with the security of God's good blessings to us. For who can imagine, if one is ruled by reason—since God has bestowed upon us the good things of this life—but that He would have us keep them for His sake? Abraham and Solomon grew rich in religion. And Job says that a good person will lay up gold as dust. But he must not be like those persons ahead of us, if they are as you describe them."

"I think that we're all agreed in this matter," Mr. Save-all said, "and therefore there's no need for more words about it."

"No, there's no need for more words about this matter indeed," Mr. Money-love added, "for a person who believes neither Scripture nor reason (and you can see we have both on our side) neither knows his own liberty nor seeks his own safety."

Mr. By-ends spoke again: "My friends, as you see, we're all going on pilgrimage. To better distract our minds from things that are bad, give me permission to set forth this question:

"Suppose a person, a minister, or a tradesperson, etc., should have an advantage lying before them to get the good blessings of this life, and find that they cannot come to them except (in appearance at least) by becoming extraordinarily fervent in some points of religion in which they haven't shown any interest before. May they not use this new interest to attain their goal, and yet be an upright and honest person?"

"I see what you're asking," said Mr. Money-love, "and with these gentlemen's permission, I'll try to answer you. First, about the minister himself. Suppose a minister, a worthy person, possesses only a small congregation or parish, yielding him only a meager income. Then it happens that he hears of a greater one by far, and has an opportunity to get it by being more studious, by preaching more frequently and fervently, and, because the temper of the people requires him to alter some of his principles—for my part, I see no reason why a person shouldn't do this, providing, of course, he has a call. In fact, I think he could do much more to advance himself and still be an honest person. Why?

A minister leaving his smaller church for a bigger one (and a bigger salary) was looked down upon by many in the seventeenth century. Mr. By-ends sees no problem with this because, he says, it is legal. Christian's counter-claim is, just because it's legal doesn't make it right.

"First, because his desire for a greater position with a larger income is certainly lawful since it's set before him by Providence. So then, he may get it if he can, asking no questions for conscience' sake.

"Second, since his desire for that more important position makes him more studious, a more fervent preacher, it makes him a better person. Yes, it makes him improve his talents, and this is certainly according to the mind of God.

"Third, as for his complying with the disposition of his people by departing from some of his principles in order to serve them, this proves that he is of a self-denying temperament and of a sweet and winning behavior, and so he is better fit for his ministerial function.

"Finally, I conclude that a minister who changes a small for a great shouldn't be judged as having wrong desires. Rather, since he has improved his talents and shown energy and diligence by it, he should be counted as one who pursues his call and the opportunity that has been put into his hand to do good.

"Now, as to the second part of your question, which concerns the tradesperson you mentioned. Suppose such a one has only a poor job, but by becoming religious may improve his lot, or perhaps get a rich wife, or more and far better, customers to his shop. For my part, I see no reason why this shouldn't lawfully be done, because, in the first place, to become religious is a virtue, no matter what a person's motive may be.

"Nor is it unlawful to get a rich wife, or more customers for one's shop. Besides, the person who gets these by becoming religious gets a good thing from good people by becoming good himself. So here's a good wife, good customers, and good gain—and all these by becoming religious, which is also good. Therefore, to become religious to get all these, is a good and profitable project."

This answer that Mr. Money-love made to Mr. By-ends's question was highly applauded by them all, and they concluded all around that it was quite wholesome and advantageous. Thinking that no one would be able to contradict this line of reasoning, and because Christian and Hopeful were still within earshot, they jointly agreed to set forth the question to them as soon as they could reach them, since they had opposed Mr. By-ends before. So they called after them to wait until they could catch up to them. They concluded among themselves, however, as they went, that Mr. Hold-the-world should set forth the question to them, because they wanted to avoid raising the heat of the argument again that had taken place with Mr. By-ends.

So they caught up with them, and after a short greeting, Mr. Hold-the-world set forth the question to Christian and his companion and invited them to answer it if they could.

Then Christian said, "Even a newcomer to religion could answer ten thousand questions like that one. For if it's unlawful to follow Christ for loaves of bread (as described in the sixth chapter of John), how much more abominable is it to make of Him and religion a stalking-horse—something used to cover one's true purpose, in order to get and enjoy the world! Nor do we find any other kind of person than heathens, hypocrites, devils, and witches who hold such opinions.

"Heathens, for when Hamor and Shechem wanted Jacob's daughter and cattle, they saw that there was no way for them to get them except by becoming circumcised. They said to their companions, 'If every male of us is circumcised as are these Hebrews, won't their livestock, their property and all their other animals become ours?' Their daughter and their cattle were what they were trying to obtain, and their religion was a stalking-horse they made use of to come at them (cf. Gen. 34:20–23).

"The hypocritical Pharisees were of the same persuasion. For a show they made lengthy prayers, but to get widow's houses was their intent, and severe punishment from God was their judgment for their misuse of religion (cf. Luke 20:46-47).

"Judas the devil was also of this opinion. He was religious in order to hold the moneybag, so that he might take what was in it (John 12:4–6), but he was lost, cast away—the man doomed to destruction (2 Thessalonians 2:3).

"Simon the Magician was of the same mind, for he wanted to have the Holy Spirit so that he might get money with the Spirit's power. His sentence from Peter's mouth was fitting (Acts 8:18–23).

"I can't get it out of my mind that a person who takes up religion for the world will throw away religion for the world; for as surely as Judas gave up the world in becoming religious, just as surely did he also sell religion and his Master for the same. To answer the question in the affirmative, as you have done, and to accept such an answer as authentic, is heathenish, hypocritical, and devilish; and you will be rewarded according to your works."

Then they stood staring at one another, but none of them had anything with which to answer Christian. Hopeful also approved of the soundness of Christian's answer, so there was a great silence among them. Mr. By-ends and his company then staggered and dropped back, so that Christian and Hopeful might go on beyond them.

Then Christian said to his companion, "If these persons can't stand before the sentence of other people, what will they do with the sentence of

God? And if they're silent when dealt with by mere humans, who are nothing but jars of clay, what will they do when they're rebuked by the flames of a consuming fire? (Hebrews 12:29)."

Then Christian and Hopeful went on ahead, leaving By-ends and his friends behind, until they came to a delicate plain called Ease. There they traveled contentedly, but the plain was narrow, so they were soon through it. At the far side of that plain was a little hill called Money-profits, and in that hill was a silver mine, which some persons who had formerly traveled that way, because of the rarity of it, had turned aside to see. But going too near the brink of the pit, the ground being treacherous under foot, they were thrown down and killed. Others had been maimed there and were unable to their dying day to be their own persons again.

Then I saw in my dream that a little off the road, over against the silver mine, stood Demas, looking like a gentleman and calling out to the passers-by to come and see. He said to Christian and his companion, "Say! Turn aside here, and I'll show you a thing or two!"

 Demas, the keeper of the Lucre silver mine, is another biblical name. The "Demas" in the Bible was a companion of the Apostle Paul for a time, but then he turned his back on Paul and, presumably, on his faith. "Lucre" means money or profits, but the usual combination is "filthy lucre," which comes from Tyndale's 1526 translation of the New Testament.

"What's so deserving as to turn us out of the Way to see it?" Christian asked.

"Here's a silver mine," replied the other, "and some people are digging in it for treasure. If you'll come, with a little effort you may richly provide for yourselves."

Then Hopeful said, "Let's go see."

"Not I," Christian said. "I've heard of this place before, and how many have been killed here. Besides that, this treasure is a trap to those who seek it, because it hinders them in their pilgrimage."

Then Christian called to Demas, saying, "Isn't the place dangerous? Hasn't it hindered many in their pilgrimage?"

"Not very dangerous," the other answered, "except to those who are careless." But Demas blushed as he spoke.

Then Christian said to Hopeful, "Let's not budge an inch, but continue on our Way."

"I'll guarantee you," Hopeful said, "that when By-ends comes up, if he has the same invitation as we, he'll turn in there to see."

"No doubt of it," Christian said. "His principles lead him that way, and the chances are a hundred to one that he'll die there."

Then Demas called again, saying, "But won't you come over and see?"

Then Christian answered vigorously, "Demas, you're an enemy to the right ways of the Lord of this Way, and you've already been condemned for turning aside by one of his Majesty's judges

(2 Timothy 4:10). Why, then, do you attempt to bring us into the same condemnation? If we turn aside at all, our Lord the King will certainly hear of it and will put us to shame there where we would like to stand with boldness before Him."

Demas shouted again that he also was one of their own kind, and if they would wait a little while, he also would walk with them himself.

Christian said, "What's your name? Isn't it the same name that I've called you?"

"Yes, my name is Demas, and I'm a son of Abraham."

"I know you," Christian said. "Gehazi was your great-grandfather (2 Kings 5:20–27) and Judas your father (Matthew 26:14-15); and you've followed in their footsteps. It's just a devilish plot you're trying to use. Your father was hanged as a traitor, and you deserve no better an end. Be assured that when we come to the King, we'll give Him word of your behavior." So they went their way.

By this time, By-ends and his companions were again in sight, and they, at the first call, went over to Demas. Now, whether they fell into the pit by looking over its brink, or whether they went down to dig, or whether they were suffocated at the bottom by the harmful gases that commonly arise, I'm not certain. But I observed this: that they were never seen again in the Way.

Now I saw that just on the other side of this plain, the Pilgrims came to a place where an old monument stood close by the highway. Seeing it, they were both concerned because of the strangeness of its form, for it seemed to them as though it was a woman transformed into the shape of a pillar. They stood looking and looking at it, but for a time they couldn't tell what they should make of it. At last, Hopeful's eye caught something written above the head of the pillar, a writing in an unusual hand. Not being a scholar, he called to Christian (for he was well educated) to see if he could pick out the meaning. Christian came, and after studying the letters a little while, found that it read like this: "Remember Lot's Wife." So he read it to his companion. They concluded that this was the pillar of salt that Lot's wife had been turned into because she looked back with a heart full of wrong desires when she was running away from Sodom for safety (Genesis 19:26). This sudden and astounding sight gave rise to this conversation.

"What a timely sight this is," Christian said. "It came to us at a fitting time after the invitation that Demas gave us to come over to view Money-profits Hill. If we had gone over, as he wanted us to do, and as you were inclining to do, my brother, we would, for all I know, have been made like this woman—a spectacle for those who come after us to look at."

Hopeful said simply, "I'm sorry that I was so foolish, and it's a wonder that I'm not now in the same condition as Lot's wife. Where was there any difference between her sin and mine? She only looked back, and I had a desire to go and see. Let grace be adored, and let me be ashamed that ever such a thing should be in my heart!"

Christian continued: "Let's take notice of what we see here, so that it might help us in the future. This woman escaped one judgment, for she didn't die when Sodom was destroyed. But she was destroyed by another judgment, because as we see, she was turned into a pillar of salt."

"True," Hopeful said. "and she may be to us both a warning and an example. A warning, so that we should stay away from her sin, or a sign of what judgment will overtake any who are not prevented by this warning. Korah, Dathan, and Abiram with the two hundred and fifty men who perished in their sin became a sign and example to others to be on guard against the same sin (Numbers 26:9-10). But above all, I'm impressed with one thing, namely, how Demas and his companions can stand so confidently back there looking for that treasure, whereas this woman, when all she did was look back, was turned into a pillar of salt. For we don't read that she stepped even one foot out of the Way, yet the judgment that came on her made her an example that's within sight of where they are, for they couldn't help seeing her if they only looked this way."

"It's a thing to be wondered at," his friend replied. "It shows that they've lost all hope. I can't tell who best to compare them to—perhaps they're like a person who picks pockets in the very presence of the judge, or who will snatch purses right under the shadow of the gallows itself. It's said of the people of Sodom that they were grievous sinners, because they were sinners before the Lord, that is, before His very eyes, regardless of the kindness that He had shown them. For the land of Sodom was like the Garden of Eden had been. This, then, provoked Him to jealousy all the more and made their plague as hot as the fire of the Lord out of heaven could make it. It is rationally to be concluded that persons such as these are, who sin in sight of and despite such examples as are set before them to warn them to the contrary, must be partakers of the severest judgments."

"Doubtless you have spoken the truth," Hopeful responded. "But what a mercy it is that neither you, but especially I, am not made the same example myself! This gives us occasion to thank God, to fear Him, and always to remember Lot's wife."

Chapter Fifteen

By-path Meadow and Doubting Castle

I saw then, that they went on their way to a pleasant river, which King David called "the streams of God" (Psalm 65:9), but John, "the river of the water of life" (Revelation 22:1). Now their way lay just on the bank of the river. Here Christian and his companion walked with great delight. They also drank of the water of the river, which was pleasant and enlivening to their weary spirits. Then, too, on the banks of this river, on either side, were green trees that bore many types of fruit, and the leaves of the tree were good for medicine (Ezekiel 47:12, Revelation 22:2). They were very delighted with the fruit of the trees, and they ate the leaves to prevent overindulging and to avoid diseases that are common to those who get overheated in traveling.

On either side of the river there was a meadow, curiously beautified with lilies and green all year long. They lay down and slept in this meadow, for here they could lie down safely. When they woke up, they gathered again from the fruit of the trees, drank again of the water of the river, and then lay down again to sleep (Psalm 23:2). They did this for several days and nights. And as they enjoyed the river, the meadow, and the fruits, they sang:

Behold how these bright crystal streams do glide
To comfort pilgrims by the highway side.
What pleasant fruit and leaves these trees do yield,
We would sell all, that we may buy this field.

So when they felt it was time to go on, they ate and drank again, and went on their way, for they were not yet at their journey's end.

Now I saw in my dream that they hadn't journeyed far until the river and the road parted for a time. They were very sorry about this, but didn't dare go out of the Way. Now the Way from the river was rough, and their feet sore because of their travels, so the souls of the pilgrims were greatly discouraged because of the Way (Numbers 21:4). Still, as they went on, they wished for a better way.

Now a little in front of them on the left side of the road there was a meadow, and a stile—a series of steps for crossing the wall to enable them to go over into it. That meadow is called By-path Meadow. Then Christian said to his companion, "If this meadow lies alongside our way, let's go over into it." He went to the stile to look, and saw a path that lay along by the way on the other side of the fence.

"It's just as I'd hoped," Christian said. "Here's the easiest going; come, good Hopeful, and let's go over."

"But what if this path should lead us out of the Way?" Hopeful asked uncertainly.

"That's not likely," the other said. "Look, doesn't it go along by the side of the way?"

So Hopeful, being persuaded by his companion, went after him over the stile. When they had gone over and had gotten onto the path, they found it very easy for their feet. On up ahead of them they caught sight of another traveler whose name was Vain-confidence. They called after him and asked him in what direction that way led.

"To the Celestial Gate," he said.

"Look," Christian said, "didn't I tell you so? By this you can see that we're right."

So they followed, and Vain-confidence went ahead of them. But the night came on, and it grew very dark, so that they lost sight of him.

Vain-confidence, not seeing the way ahead, fell into a deep pit (Isaiah 9:16) that was made there on purpose by the prince of those grounds to catch boastful fools with it, and was dashed to pieces with his fall.

Now Christian and Hopeful heard him fall. So they called out to know what was happening, but there was no answer. All they heard was groaning.

Then Hopeful said, "Where are we now?"

His fellow traveler said nothing, afraid that he had led his brother out of the Way. Now it began to rain and thunder and lightning in a very dreadful manner, and the water rose at great speed.

Hopeful groaned in himself, saying, "Oh, if only I had kept on my way!"

"But who could have thought that this path should have led us out of the Way?" Christian asked defensively.

"I was afraid of it at the very beginning," Hopeful said. "I gave you that gentle caution. I wish now I had spoken more plainly, and I would have if you hadn't been older than I."

"Good brother, don't be offended," Christian replied. "I'm sorry I've brought you out of the Way and that I've put you into such imminent danger. Forgive me, my brother. I didn't do it out of any evil intent."

"Be comforted, my brother, for I forgive you," Hopeful said. "Believe, too, that this will be for our good."

Christian spoke again. "I am glad I have a merciful brother with me. But we mustn't stand here. Let's try to get back to the Way again."

"Let me go in front, brother," Hopeful said.

"No," Christian said, "you must let me go first, so that if there's any danger, I may be in it first, because it was by my counsel that we both went out of the Way."

"No," Hopeful said, "you won't go first, for your mind is troubled and it may lead you out of the Way again."

Then, for their encouragement, they heard the voice of one saying, "Take note of the highway, the road that you take. Return" (Jeremiah 31:21).

But by this time, the waters had risen greatly, and the way of going back was very dangerous indeed. Then I thought that it's easier to go out of the Way when we're in it, than to go back when we're out. Yet they dared to go back, but it was so dark and the flood was so high that in their returning they almost drowned nine or ten times.

They were unable, with all the skill they had, to get back to the stile that night. So at last, resting under a little shelter, they sat down there to wait for dawn to break. But being weary, they fell asleep.

Now there was, not far from the place where they lay, a castle called Doubting Castle, whose owner was Giant Despair. It was in his grounds they were now sleeping. Getting up early in the morning and walking up and down in his fields, Giant Despair caught Christian and Hopeful asleep. With a grim and surly voice, he woke them up and asked them where they came from and what they were doing in his grounds. They told him they were pilgrims and that they had lost their way. Then the Giant said, "You have trespassed on my grounds tonight, and therefore you must go along with me."

So they were forced to go because he was stronger than they. They had little to say, for they knew themselves to be at fault. The Giant, therefore, drove them before him, and put them into his castle in a very dark dungeon, nasty and stinking to the spirits of these two men (Psalm 88:18). Here they lay from Wednesday morning till Saturday night without one bit of bread or drop of drink, or light, or anyone to ask how they were doing. They were in a very bad state, far from friends and acquaintance. And in this condition, Christian had the double sorrow of knowing that it was through his unwise counsel that they had been brought into this distress.

Now Giant Despair had a wife, and her name was Distrust. So when he had gone to bed, he told his wife what he had done—that he had taken a couple of prisoners and cast them into his dungeon for trespassing his grounds. He asked her what he should do further to them. So she asked him what they were, where they came from, and where they were headed, and he told her. Then she counseled him that when he arose in the morning he should beat them without any mercy. So, when he arose the next day, he got a terrible crab-tree club and went down into the dungeon to them, and there began first to scold them at length as if they were dogs, although they never gave him a word to annoy him. Then he jumped on them and beat them fearfully, in such a way that they weren't able to help themselves, or even to turn themselves over on the floor. This done, he withdrew and left them to express sorrow for their misery and to mourn under their distress. So all that day they spent the time in nothing but sighs and bitter expressions of grief.

The next night, Distrust, talking with her husband about them further and finding that they were still alive, advised him to counsel them to do away with themselves. So when morning came, he went to them in a surly manner as before, and perceiving that they were very sore with the blows he had given them the day before, he told them that since they were never likely to get out of that place, their only hope was to make an end of themselves, either with knife, rope, or poison. "For why," said he, "should you choose life, seeing it is attended with so much bitterness?"

But they begged him to let them go. With that he looked fiercely at them, and rushing at them would doubtless have made an end of them himself, but instead fell into one of his fits, which he sometimes did in sunny weather, and for a time lost the use of his head. Therefore he withdrew and left them as before to consider what to do. Then the prisoners consulted between themselves about whether it was best to take his counsel or not. This is how their conversation went:

 Today, we might call Despair and Distrust by another name: Depression. As the leading cause of suicide, untreated depression is a real problem in our world, and Bunyan gives voice to some suicidal thoughts. It makes me wonder if he thought about suicide during his own imprisonment.

"Brother," Christian said, "what shall we do? The life that we now live is miserable. For my part, I don't know whether it's best to live this way or to die immediately. 'I prefer strangling and death' (Job 7:15), and the grave is easier for me than this dungeon. Should we let ourselves be ruled by this Giant?"

"Our present condition is dreadful indeed," his companion answered. "Death would be far more welcome to me than to remain this way forever. Yet, let us consider, the Lord of the country to which we are going has said, 'You shall not murder" (Exodus 20:13), no, not anyone else; much more, then, are we forbidden to take this giant's counsel to kill ourselves. Besides, one who kills another can commit murder only to his body. But for one to kill himself, is to kill body and soul at once. Furthermore, my brother, you talk of the ease of the grave; but have you forgotten the hell to which murderers are certain to go? For 'no murderers have eternal life in them' (1 John 3:15).

"And let's consider again that the whole law isn't in the hand of Giant Despair. Others, as far as I can understand, have been taken by him as well as we, and yet have escaped out of his hand. Who knows but that God who made the world might cause Giant Despair to die? Or that some time or other he might forget to lock us in? Or that he might, in a short time, have another of his fits in front of us and might lose the use of his old limbs? And if that should ever happen again, for my part, I'm resolved to gather my courage and to try my utmost to get out from under his hand. I was a fool that I didn't try to do it before, but nonetheless, my brother, let's be patient and endure a while. The time may come that may give us a happy release. But let's not be our own murderers."

With these words, Hopeful was able to moderate the mind of his brother, so they continued together in the dark that day, in their sad and mournful condition.

Well, toward evening, the Giant went down into the dungeon again to see if his prisoners had taken his counsel. But when he came to them he found them alive; and truly, alive was all, for now, for lack of bread and water, and because of the wounds they had received under his beating, they could do little else but breathe. But, I say, he found them alive. At this, he fell into a dreadful rage and told them that since they had disobeyed his counsel, it would be worse for them than if they had never been born.

At this they trembled greatly, and I think that Christian fainted; but coming a little to himself again, they renewed their conversation about the Giant's counsel, and about whether even now they had better take it or not. Now Christian again seemed to be for doing it, but Hopeful again made reply, as follows:

"My brother," he said, "don't you remember how valiant and brave you've been up till now? Apollyon couldn't crush you, nor could all that you heard or saw or felt in the Valley of the Shadow of Death. What hardship, terror, and amazement you've already gone through! And are you now nothing but fear? You see that I'm in the dungeon with you, a far weaker person by nature than you are. Also, this Giant has wounded me as well as you, and has cut off the bread and water from my mouth; and with you I mourn without the light. But let's exercise a little more patience! Remember how courageous you were at Vanity Fair and were afraid neither of the chain, nor the cage, nor yet of a bloody death. Then let's at least avoid the shame that is so unbecoming for a Christian to be found in, and bear up with patience as well as we can."

Now night had come again, and the Giant and his wife were in bed again when she asked him about the prisoners and if they had taken his counsel. He replied, "They're sturdy rascals. They choose to bear every hardship rather than to do away with themselves."

Then she said, "Take them into the castle yard tomorrow, and show them the bones and skulls of those that you have already dispatched, and make them believe that before a week comes to an end, you'll also tear them in pieces as you have done those who came before them."

So when the morning came, the Giant went to them again and took them into the castle yard, and showed them, as his wife had suggested to him. "These," he said, "were once pilgrims as you are, and they trespassed on my grounds as you have done. And when I thought fit, I tore them in pieces, and so, within ten days, I will do the same to you! Go! Get down to your den again!" And with that, he beat them all the way back to the dungeon. They lay, therefore, all day on Saturday in as lamentable state as before.

Now when night had come, and when Mrs. Distrust and her husband the Giant had gotten into bed, they began to renew their discussion concerning their prisoners. And the old Giant wondered why he could neither by blows nor by counsel bring them to an end. With that, his wife replied: "I'm afraid," she said, "that they live in hope that someone will come to rescue them, or that they have lock-picking tools about them by means of which they hope to escape."

"And do you say so, my dear?" the Giant said. "Then I'll search them in the morning."

Well, on Saturday about midnight, they began to pray, and continued in prayer almost till day-break.

Now, a little before it was day, good Christian, as though half-amazed, broke out in this passionate speech: "What a fool I am," he said, "to lie like this in a stinking dungeon when I might as well walk at liberty! I have a key in my chest pocket, called Promise, that will, I am persuaded, open any lock in Doubting Castle."

Then Hopeful said, "That's good news, good brother; take it out of your chest pocket and try!"

Then Christian pulled it out of his chest pocket, and began to try at the dungeon door. The bolt of the door, as he turned the key, gave way and the door flew open with ease, and both Christian and Hopeful came out of the dungeon. Then Christian went to the outer door that led into the castle yard, and with his key opened that door also. After this he went to the iron gate, for that too had to be opened. That lock went damnably hard, yet the key did open it. They flung open the gate to make their escape with speed, but that gate made such a creaking noise as it opened that it woke up Giant Despair, who rose hastily to pursue his prisoners. But the Giant felt his limbs fail as his fits took him again, and so he could by no means go after them! Then they went on and came to the King's highway, and so were safe, because they were out of the jurisdiction of the Giant.

 We do, indeed, know more about depression today than John Bunyan did, so it might seem a little too easy to get past suicidal thoughts by finding a Promise in your pocket.

Now when they got over the stile, they began to consider what they could do at that stile to prevent others who came after them from falling into the hands of Giant Despair. They agreed to erect a marker there and to engrave this sentence on the side of it: "Over this stile is the way to Doubting

Castle, which is kept by Giant Despair, who despises the King of the Celestial Country and seeks to destroy His holy pilgrims." Many, therefore, who came after, read what was written and escaped the danger. Having erected the marker, they went on their way, singing,

> *Out of the way we went and found*
> *We tread upon forbidden ground.*
> *Let them who follow have a care,*
> *Lest heedlessness make them unaware,*
> *And they in Doubting Castle fare*
> *As prisoners of the Giant Despair.*

Chapter Sixteen

The Pilgrims Reach the Delectable Mountains

Christian and Hopeful continued on their way till they came to the Delectable Mountains, which belong to the Lord of the hill of which we have spoken before. So they went up to the mountains to look at the gardens and orchards, the vineyards and fountains of water. There they drank and washed themselves and ate freely of the vineyards.

Now on the tops of these mountains there were Shepherds feeding their flocks, and they stood by the side of the highway. The pilgrims went to them, and leaning on their staffs (as is common with weary pilgrims when they stand to talk with anyone by the road), they asked, "Whose Delectable Mountains are these? And whose are the sheep that feed on them?"

The gentle shepherds of the Delectable Mountains cause us immediately to think of the shepherds who visited the baby Jesus in the manger.

"These mountains are Immanuel's Land," the Shepherds replied. "And they are within sight of His city. The sheep are His, too, and He laid down His life for them" (John 10:11).

"Is this the way to the Celestial City?" Christian queried. "Indeed," replied the Shepherds, "you are right on your way."

"And how far is it from here?" Christian asked.

"Too far for any but those who shall arrive there indeed," was the answer.

"Is the Way safe or dangerous?"

"Safe for those for whom it is safe," was the answer; "but the rebellious stumble in them" (Hosea 14:9).

Christian continued his inquiry: "Is there, in this place, any relief for Pilgrims who are weary in the Way?"

The Shepherd replied, "The Lord of these mountains has charged us not to 'forget to show hospitality to strangers' (Hebrews 13:2), so, the good of the country is before you."

The Shepherds saw that they were traveling on foot, and began to ask them the same questions that others had asked along their pilgrimage, such as, "Where did you come from? How did you get into the Way? And by what means have you so persevered in the Way? For only a few of those who begin on pilgrimage ever reach these mountains," they said sadly. But when the Shepherds had heard their answers, they were pleased with them, and looked very lovingly on them, saying, "Welcome to the Delectable Mountains."

The names of the Shepherds are Knowledge, Experience, Watchful, and Sincere. They took the Pilgrims by the hand and led them to their tents, making them partake of food that was ready for them to eat. They said to them, "We wish that you would stay here awhile, to be acquainted with us, and even more, to take comfort in the good of these Delectable Mountains."

Christian and Hopeful said that they were content to stay, so they went to their rest that night, because it was very late.

The next morning the Shepherds called Christian and Hopeful to walk with them on the mountains. So they went out with them and walked awhile, having a pleasant view on every side. Then the Shepherds said to one another, "Shall we show these Pilgrims some wonders?" So when they had concluded that they should do it, they took them first to the top of a hill called Error, which was very steep on its furthest side, and told them to look down at the bottom. As Christian and Hopeful looked down, they saw at the bottom several persons dashed all to pieces by a fall they'd had from the top.

"What does this mean?" asked Christian.

The Shepherds answered, "Haven't you heard of those who were led into error by listening to Hymenaeus and Philetus, concerning the resurrection of the body? (2 Timothy 2:17-18)."

Hymenaeus and Philetus wrongly preached that the resurrection of the body had already happened. The correct Christian teaching is that the resurrection will take place when Christ returns at the end of time.

They answered, "Yes."

Then the Shepherds continued, "Those you see dashed in pieces at the bottom of this mountain are the ones; and they have remained unburied to this day, as you see, for an example to others to take care how they climb too high, or how they come too near the edge of this mountain."

They went on to the top of another mountain, the name of which is Caution, and told them to look far off. When they did this, they thought they saw several persons walking up and down among the tombs they could see in the distance. They could tell, as they watched, that the persons were blind, because they stumbled on the tombs and gravestones as they walked, and couldn't find their way out from them.

"What does this mean?" Christian asked.

"Didn't you see a little below these mountains a stile that led into a meadow on the left side of this Way?" the Shepherds asked.

They answered, "Yes."

Then the Shepherds said, "From that stile there goes a path that leads directly to Doubting Castle, which is kept by Giant Despair, and these people (pointing to the ones among the tombs) came once on pilgrimage as you do now, till they came to that same stile. And because the right Way was rough in that place, they chose to go out of it into that meadow, and there they were taken by Giant Despair, cast into Doubting Castle, and after they had been kept in the dungeon, he put their eyes out and led them among these tombs, where he has left them to wander to this very day. This is to fulfill the saying, 'Whoever strays from the path of prudence comes to rest in the company of the dead'" (Proverbs 21:16).

Then Christian and Hopeful looked at one another, with tears running down their cheeks, but said nothing to the Shepherds.

Then I saw in my dream that the Shepherds took them to another place, where there was a door in the side of a hill. They opened the door and invited them to look in. They saw within that it was very dark and smoky, and they thought that they heard a rumbling noise, like that of fire, and a cry of some tormented persons, and thought that they smelled the scent of hot sulfur.

Then Christian said, "What does this mean?"

The Shepherds told them, "This is a side road to hell, a way that hypocrites go in; for instance, those who sell their birthright, as Esau did (Genesis 25:29–34); those who sell their Master, as Judas did; those who blaspheme the Gospel, as Alexander did (2 Timothy 4:14); and who lie and deceive, with Ananias and Sapphira (Acts 5:1–5)."

Then Hopeful observed to the Shepherds: "I see that all these had on them the appearance of pilgrims, as we have now, didn't they?"

"Yes, and they kept it a long time, too," the Shepherds answered.

"How far might they have gone on in pilgrimage in their day, since they were, in spite of their travels, cast away so miserably?"

"Some further, and some not so far as these mountains," was the reply.

Then the Pilgrims said one to another, "We need to cry to the Strong One for strength."

"Indeed," the Shepherds said, "and you will need to use it when you have it, too!"

By this time, the Pilgrims wanted to go on, and the Shepherds agreed that they should, so they walked together toward the end of the mountains. Then the Shepherds said to one another, "Here let's show the Pilgrims the gates of the Celestial City, if they have the skill to look through our telescope. The Pilgrims were happy to accept the suggestion, so they led them to the top of a high hill, called Clear, and gave them their telescope to look through.

Then they tried to look, but the remembrance of the last thing that the Shepherds had shown them made their hands tremble, so that they couldn't look steadily through the glass. Yet they thought they saw something like the gate and also some of the glory of the place.

When they were about to start out, one of the Shepherds gave them a sketch of the Way. Another told them to beware of the Flatterer. A third warned them to take care not to sleep on the Enchanted Ground. And a fourth wished them well on their journey.

And so the Pilgrims went on their way.

Chapter Seventeen

Ignorance and Little-faith

The Pilgrims went down the mountains along the highway toward the Celestial City. Now, a little below these mountains, on the left side, lies the country of Conceit. From that country there was a little crooked lane coming into the road on which the Pilgrims were walking. Here they met a very brisk young man who came out of that country, whose name was Ignorance. So Christian asked him where he was coming from, and where he was headed.

"Sir, I was born in the country that lies off there a little on the left side," the young man answered, "and I'm going to the Celestial City."

"But how do you think you'll get in at the gate?" Christian asked. "You may find some difficulty there."

"I would get in as other good people do," he said.

Christian continued, "But what do you have to show at that gate, that may cause the gate to be opened for you?"

Ignorance replied, "I know my Lord's will, and I've lived a good life. I pay everyone what is due them, I pray, fast, pay tithes, and give alms, and I've left my country for the one to which I'm going."

The young man Ignorance reminds us of a couple people who approached Jesus during his ministry. For instance, the rich young man of Matthew 19—he was obeying all of God's laws, but when Jesus told him to sell everything and give the money to the poor, the young man "went away sad." Christian makes it clear that Ignorance is doomed because the only way to the Celestial City is through the Narrow Gate (with the exception of Hopeful!).

Christian persisted: "But you didn't come in at the narrow gate at the start of the Way! You came in through that same crooked lane there, and I'm afraid that no matter what you may think of yourself, when the day of reckoning comes, you'll have it laid to your charge that you're a thief and a robber, instead of gaining admittance to the City" (John 10:1).

"Gentlemen, you are utter strangers to me, and I don't know you," Ignorance replied condescendingly. "Please be content to follow the religion of your country, and I'll follow the religion of mine. I hope all will be well. And as for that gate you talk of, the whole world knows that it's a great distance from our country. I can't believe that anyone in all our area so much as knows the way to it, nor do they need to care whether they do or not, since we have, as you see, a fine, pleasant green lane that comes down from our country, the nearest route into this Way."

When Christian saw that the man was "wise in his own conceit," he whispered to Hopeful, "There's more hope for a fool than for him" (Proverbs 26:12). And he added, "Even as fools walk along the road, they lack sense, and show everyone how stupid they are (Ecclesiastes 10:3). Shall we talk further with him, or leave him behind right now to think over what he's already heard, and then stop again to speak to him afterward, to see if in any way we might do him any good?"

Hopeful said, "I don't think it's good to say everything to him at once. Let's pass him by, if you will, and talk to him later on, even as he's able to bear it."

So they both went on, and Ignorance followed behind. When they had gone a little way, they entered into a very dark lane, where they met a person whom seven devils had bound with seven strong cords; and they were carrying him back to the door that they had seen on the side of the hill (Matthew 12:45). Now good Christian began to tremble again, as did his companion Hopeful. Yet as the devils led the man away, Christian looked to see if he knew him. He thought it might be Turn-away, who lived in the town of Apostasy. But he didn't see his face clearly, for the man's head hung down like that of a thief who's been caught. After he had passed, however, Hopeful looked back and saw on the man's back a paper with this writing: "Professed the faith but rebelled and damnably abandoned it."

As they went on, Christian remarked to his companion, "I remember what was told me of something that happened to a good person in this area. His name was Little-faith, but he was a good man and lived in the town of Sincere. What happened was this: At the entrance of this passage there came down from Broadway Gate a lane called Dead Man's Lane, so called because of the murders that occurred there so often. Little-faith was going on pilgrimage, as we're now doing, and chanced to sit down there and fell asleep. Now it happened at that time that there came down the lane from Broadway Gate, three sturdy scoundrels—Faint-heart, Mistrust, and Guilt. They were brothers, and catching sight of Little-faith as he sat there, they came galloping up with all speed. He was just waking up, getting ready to resume his journey. So they all rushed to him and with threatening language told him to stand up. At this Little-faith looked white as a ghost, and had neither the strength to fight or to run away. Then Faint-heart said, 'Hand over your wallet.'

Here's a story-within-the-story. Christian tells Hopeful a parable of a man who made it to the Celestial City, but because he did so with little faith, he missed many of the blessings along the way. It's similar to a parable Jesus told about a master who left his servants with talents; you can read about it in Matthew 25:14–30.

"Little-faith cried out, 'Thieves! Thieves!' And with that, Guilt, with a huge club that was in his hand, struck Little-faith on the head, and with that blow, felled him flat to the ground, where he lay bleeding as though he would bleed to death. All this while the thieves stood by. But at last, hearing someone on the road, and fearing that it might be Great-grace, who lives in the city of Good-confidence, they took to their heels, and left this good man to shift for himself. Now after a while, Little-faith came to himself, and got up and began to scramble on his way again. That was the story I heard."

"Did they take from him everything he had?" Hopeful asked.

"No," Christian said. "The place where his jewels were they never ransacked, so he still kept those. But as I was told, the good man was very much grieved at his loss, because the thieves got most of his spending money. What they didn't get, as I said, were jewels. He also had a little odd money left, but hardly enough to bring him to his journey's end. No, if I was not misinformed, he was forced to beg as he went, to keep himself alive. He wasn't free to sell his jewels. But he had to beg and do what he could, and he often went with a hungry belly the greater part of the rest of the way."

"But isn't it a wonder that they didn't get from him his certificate by which he was to be admitted to the Celestial City?" Hopeful asked.

"It is a wonder," the other said. "But they didn't get that, though they didn't miss it through any cleverness of his; for he, so dismayed by their coming upon him, had neither the power nor the skill to hide anything. So it was more by good Providence than by any endeavor of his that they missed any good thing."

"But it must be a comfort to him that they didn't get his jewels from him," Hopeful observed.

"It might have been great comfort to him if he had used it as he ought," said Christian. "But those who told me the story said that he made very little use of it, all the rest of the way, and that because of his dismay in losing his money, he forgot the fact that they hadn't stolen his jewels for most of the rest of his journey. And they said that when at any time the occurrence came to his mind and he began to be comforted with what was not lost, fresh thoughts of his loss would come on him again, and those thoughts would swallow him up.

"Alas! Poor man!" Hopeful exclaimed. "This could be nothing other than a great grief to him."

"Grief! Yes, a grief indeed." Christian shook his head sadly. Wouldn't it have been so to any of us if we had been robbed and wounded as he was—and in that strange place, too? It's a wonder he didn't die with grief, poor heart. I was told that he spent almost all the rest of the way uttering nothing but grief-filled, bitter complaints, telling all who overtook him in the Way, where he was robbed and how, who they were who did it, and what he lost, how he was wounded, and that he hardly escaped with his life."

Hopeful spoke again. "Isn't it a wonder that his need didn't make him decide to sell or pawn some of his jewels, so that he might have what he needed to make his journey more tolerable?"

"You talk like one with a shell on his head to this very day!" Christian retorted. "In exchange for what would he pawn them, or to whom should he sell them? In all that country where he was robbed, his jewels were not valued, nor did he desire the relief that could be gained from such a bargain. Besides, if his jewels had been missing when he arrived at the gate of the Celestial City, he would have been excluded from an inheritance there, and that would have been worse to him than the appearance and villainy of ten thousand thieves, and that he knew well enough!"

"Why are you so sharp, my brother?" Hopeful asked. "Esau sold his birthright, and that for a mere bowl of stew, and that birthright was his greatest jewel (Hebrews 12:16). If he did that, why might not Little-faith do so too?"

Christian replied, "Esau did sell his birthright indeed, and so do many besides him. By so doing they exclude themselves from the chief blessing, as that despicable man did. But you must see a difference between Esau and Little-faith, and also between their conditions. Esau's belly was his god, but Little-faith's belly was not. Esau's need lay in his fleshly appetite; Little-faith's did not. Besides, Esau could see no further than to the fulfilling of his lusts: 'Look, I am about to die. What good is the birthright to me?' (Genesis 25:32).

"But Little-faith, though it was his lot to have only a little faith, was kept by his little faith from such extravagances, and was made to see and prize his jewels too much to sell them as Esau sold his birthright. You don't read anywhere that Esau had faith, no, not so much as a little. Therefore it's no marvel, where only the flesh bears sway, as it will in any person where there is no faith to resist it, if he should sell his birthright, his soul and everything—and that to the devil of hell! For such persons are like wild donkeys, as Jeremiah reminds us (Jeremiah 2:24). When their minds are set on their lusts they will have them, whatever the cost.

"But Little-faith was of another temperament. His mind was on divine things. His livelihood was on things that were spiritual and from above. Therefore to what end would one who is of such a disposition sell his jewels, even if there had been anyone to buy them, to fill his mind with empty things? Will a person give a penny to fill his stomach with hay, or can you persuade the dove to live on garbage like the crow? Though faithless ones can, for their fleshly lusts, pawn or mortgage or sell what they have and themselves outright to boot, yet those who have faith, saving faith—

though only a little of it—can't do so. Here, my brother, is your mistake!"

When Christian ceased his speaking, Hopeful looked at him and spoke again. "I acknowledge my mistake, but your severe words almost made me angry!"

Christian smiled. "Why, I only compared you to some of the birds of the brisker sort, who will run to and fro with a shell on their heads. But pass that by, and consider the matter under discussion and all will be well between you and me."

"But, Christian, these three fellows, I'm sure in my heart, are only a company of cowards," Hopeful said. "Would they otherwise have run, do you think, as they did when they heard the sound of someone approaching on the road? Why didn't Little-faith pluck up more courage? He might, I think, have stood one encounter with them and then yield, if there was no other remedy."

"Many have said they are cowards," his brother answered. "But few have found it so in the time of trial. As for courage, Little-faith had none. I gather from what you say, my brother, that you're ready for a fight and then to yield. Since that is 'the height of your stomach,' as they say, even now when they're at a distance from you, you might have second thoughts if suddenly they should appear to you as they did to him.

"But consider again, they're just traveling thieves; they serve under the king of the bottomless pit, who will, if he has to, come to their aid himself, and his voice is as the roaring of a lion (1 Peter 5:8). I myself have been attacked as this Little-faith was, and I found it a terrible thing. These three villains set upon me, and when I began, like a Christian, to resist, all they had to do was give a call and in came their master. I would, as the saying is, have given my life for a penny. But as God would have it, I was clothed with strong armor. But even though I was so equipped, I found it hard work to show courage. No one can tell what in that combat may be in store for us except one who's been in the battle himself."

Hopeful was persistent. "But they ran, you see, when they only supposed that Great-grace was on the way."

"That's true," Christian said. "They've often fled, both they and their master, when Great-grace appeared. But that's no wonder, for he's the King's Champion. But I think you'll recognize some difference between Little-faith and the King's Champion. All the King's subjects aren't His champions, nor can they do such feats of war as He when they're tested. Is it fitting to think that a young boy should handle Goliath as David did? Or that there should be the strength of an ox in a wren? Some are strong, some are weak. Some have great faith, some have little. This man was one of the weak, and because of it, he went to the wall."

"I wish it had been Great-grace for the sake of those scoundrels!" Hopeful exclaimed.

Christian saw that he had not yet gotten his point across. "Even if it had been, he might have had his hands full," he said. "I must tell you that, though Great-grace is excellent in using his weapons, and that as long as he keeps them at sword's point can do well enough with them, yet, if Faint-heart, Mistrust, or Guilt get very close to him, it goes hard with him, and they'll knock him down. Anyone who looks carefully on Great-grace's face will see scars and cuts there that easily show what I say. I heard that he once said, and that when he was in combat, 'We despaired of life itself' (2 Corinthians 1:8). How did those strong scoundrels and their fellows make David groan, mourn, and roar? Peter, you remember, said he would be faithful to the end. Yet though some call him the prince of the apostles, these scoundrels handled him so that in the end they made him afraid of a young woman (Mark 14:66-72).

"Besides, their king is at their whistle-call. He's never out of hearing, and if at any time they're getting the worst of it, he will, if possible, come to help them. Of him it is said, 'The sword that reaches him has no effect, nor does the spear or the dart or the javelin. He treats iron like straw and bronze like rotten wood. Arrows do not make him flee; slingstones are like chaff to him. A clubs seems to him but a piece of straw; he laughs at the rattling of the lance' (cf. Job 41:26–29).

"What can a person do in this case? It's true, if a person could at every turn have Job's horse, and had skill and courage to ride it, he might do notable things: 'Do you give the horse its strength or clothe its neck with a flowing mane? Do you make it leap like a locust, striking terror with its proud snorting? It paws fiercely, rejoicing in its strength, and charges into the fray. It laughs at fear, afraid of nothing; it does not shy away from the sword. The quiver rattles against its side, along with the flashing spear and lance. In frenzied excitement it eats up the ground; it cannot stand still when the trumpet sounds. At the blast of the trumpet it snorts, "Aha!" It catches the scent of battle from afar, the shout of commanders and the battle cry' (Job 39:19–25).

"But for such lowly servants as you and I are, let's never desire to meet with an enemy, nor brag as though we could do better when we hear that others have been thwarted, nor be pleased at the thoughts of our own human strength! For such persons commonly come off the worst when they're tested. Look at Peter, whom I mentioned before. He swaggered—yes, he would, he would, as his proud mind prompted him to say, he would do better and stand more for his Master than everyone else. But who was as defeated and run down by these villains as he was?

"When we hear that such robberies are done on the King's highway, two things are appropriate for us to do: first, to go out armored and to be sure to take a shield with us; for it was for lack of that, that the one who attacked Leviathan, as I described earlier from the book of Job, couldn't make him yield. Indeed, if we don't have our shield, he's not at all afraid of us. Therefore another has said, 'In addition to all this, take up the shield of faith, with which you can extinguish all the flaming arrows of the evil one' (Ephesians 6:16).

"It's good, too (in the second place), that we ask the King for a convoy, yes, that He will go with us Himself. This made David rejoice when he was in the Valley of the Shadow of Death; and Moses was rather for dying where he stood than go one step without his God (Exodus 33:15). Oh, my brother, if He will only go along with us, what need is there to be afraid of tens of thousands who assail us on every side? (Psalm 3:6). But without Him, the proud helpers 'fall among the slain' (Isaiah 10:4).

"For my part, I've been in the battle before now; and although I'm still alive, as you see, through the goodness of the One who is best, I can't boast of my courage in battle. I'll be glad if I meet with no more such assaults, although I'm afraid we haven't gotten beyond all danger. However, since the lion and the bear haven't devoured me yet, I have hope that God will also deliver us from the next enemy (1 Samuel 17:37)."

Chapter Eighteen

The Pilgrims Learn a Lesson the Hard Way

So they went on and Ignorance followed. They went then till they came to a place where they saw a road dividing off from their Way. Both ways seemed to lie straight, and they didn't know which way to take. So they stood still to consider. As they were thinking about the way, a man covered with a very light-colored robe came to them and asked them why they were standing there. They answered that they were going to the Celestial City, but didn't know which of these ways to take.

"Follow me," said the man, "because that's where I'm going."

So they followed him in the way that divided off from the Way in which they were traveling. As they went, the road turned and turned by degrees, so that before they knew it, their faces were turned away from the City. Yet they followed him. But by and by, before they were aware, he led them both within reach of a net in which they both became so entangled that they didn't know what to do. With that, the white robe fell off the man's back, and they saw where they were. They lay there crying for some time, for they couldn't get themselves out.

Then Christian said to his companion, "Now I see my error. Didn't the Shepherds tell us to beware of the flatterers? As in the saying of the wise, so we have found it to be true today, 'Those who flatter their neighbor are spreading nets for their feet' (Proverbs 29:5)."

"They also gave us a sketch of directions about the Way," Hopeful remembered. "But somehow we forgot to look at it, and didn't keep ourselves from the paths of the destroyer. Here David was wiser than we are; for he says, 'I have kept myself from the ways of the violent through what your lips have commanded' (Psalm 17:4)."

They lay like this, crying over their being caught in the net. At last they caught sight of a Shining One coming toward them with a whip of small cords in his hand. When he had reached the place where they were, he asked them where they had come from and what they were doing there. They told him that they were poor Pilgrims going to Zion, but had been led out of their Way by a man clothed in white who told them follow him, saying that he too was going to Mount Zion.

Then the Shining One said, "It's the Flatterer, a false apostle who has transformed himself into an angel of light" (2 Corinthians 11:13-14). So he tore open the net and let the men out. Then he said to them, "Follow me, so that I may set you in your way again." He led them back to the Way that they had left to follow the Flatterer.

"Where did you sleep last night?" the Shining One asked. They said, "With the Shepherds, on the Delectable Mountains."

He asked them then if they hadn't received from those Shepherds a note of direction for the road.

They answered, "Yes."

"But did you," he said, "when you were at a standstill, pull out and read your note?"

They answered, "No."

He asked them, "Why?"

They said, "We forgot."

He asked them, "Didn't the Shepherds warn you to beware of the Flatterer?"

They answered, "Yes, but we didn't imagine that this fine-spoken man could have been the Flatterer" (Romans 16:18).

Then I saw in my dream that he commanded them to lie down; when they did this, he punished them severely with his whip, to teach them the good Way in which they should walk; and as he punished them, he said, "Those whom I love, I rebuke and discipline. So be earnest, and repent" (Revelation 3:19). Having done this, he told them to go on their way, and to take good care to follow the other directions of the Shepherds. So they thanked him for all his kindness, and went quietly along the right way, singing:

To be honest, I think this is the strangest paragraph in the whole book. This angel whips the Pilgrims, and they thank him for his kindness! This is a bizarre way for God to show love.

> *Come higher, you that walk along the Way*
> *See how the Pilgrims fare who go astray!*
> *When they good counsel lightly did forget*
> *They soon were caught within the Flatterer's net.*
> *God rescued them again, but yet you see,*
> *They're flogged as well. Let this your warning be!*

Now, after a while they saw afar off someone coming quietly and alone toward them. Christian said to his fellow, "Over there is a person with his back toward Zion, and he's coming to meet us.

"I see him," Hopeful said. "Let's be careful now, in case he should also prove to be a flatterer."

The man drew nearer and nearer, and at last he came up to them. His name was Atheist, and he asked them where they were headed.

"We're going to Mount Zion," Christian replied. Then Atheist fell into a very great laughter.

"What's the meaning of your laughter?" Christian asked. "I'm laughing to see what ignorant persons you are," the other replied scornfully, "to take upon you so tedious a journey, and yet you're likely to have nothing but your travel for your pains."

"Why," Christian asked, "do you think we won't be allowed in?"

"Allowed in!" His voice carried contempt as he spoke. "There is no such place as you dream of in all this world."

"But there is in the world to come," Christian said.

Atheist went on: "When I was at home in my own country, I heard what you now maintain to be true, and from that hearing went out to see. I've been looking for this city for twenty years, but I find no more of it than I did the first day I set out" (Ecclesiastes 10:15).

"But we've both heard and believe that there is such a place to be found," Christian said.

Atheist shook his head. "If I hadn't believed when I was at home, I wouldn't have come this far to search. But since I've found nothing (and certainly I would have if there were any such place to be found, for I've gone in search of it further than you), I'm going back again and will attempt to refresh myself with the things that I threw away then, for hopes of what I now see doesn't exist."

Then Christian said to Hopeful, his companion, "Is it true, what this man has said?"

"Watch out!" Hopeful said. "He's one of the flatterers. Remember what it cost us once already for listening to that kind of person. What? No Mount Zion? From the Delectable Mountains didn't we see the gate of the city? And aren't we now supposed to walk by faith (2 Corinthians 5:7)? Let's go on," Hopeful said, "for fear that the man with the whip will overtake us again. You should have taught me this lesson, which I will now return to you: 'Stop listening to instruction, my child, and you will stray from the words of knowledge' (Proverbs 19:27). I say, my brother, stop listening to that man, and let us 'believe and be saved' (Hebrews 10:39)."

Christian smiled at Hopeful. "I didn't ask you the question because I doubted the truth of our belief myself, but to test you and to draw from you the fruit of the honesty of your heart. As for this person, I know that his mind has been blinded by the god of this age (2 Corinthians 4:4). Let's go on, you and I, knowing that we believe the truth, and no lie comes from the truth' (1 John 2:21)."

Hopeful replied, "I rejoice in hope of the glory of God."

So they turned away from the man, and he, still laughing at them, went his way.

Chapter Nineteen

Hopeful's Testimony

I saw then in my dream that they went on till they came to a certain country where the air naturally tended to make strangers drowsy as they came into it. Here Hopeful began to be very sluggish and sleepy, and said to Christian, "I'm beginning to grow so drowsy that I can scarcely hold up my eyelids. Let's lie down here and take a nap."

"By no means!" Christian replied sharply. "For fear that by sleeping we will never wake again!"

"Why, my brother?" Hopeful asked. "Sleep is sweet to one who labors. We may be refreshed if we take a nap."

Christian looked at him sternly. "Don't you remember that one of the Shepherds warned us us to beware of the Enchanted Ground? He meant by that that we should beware of sleeping. 'So then, let us not be like others, who are asleep, but let us be awake and sober' (1 Thessalonians 5:6)."

"I acknowledge that I'm wrong," Hopeful said, smiling. "If I'd been here alone, I would have, by sleeping, run the danger of death. I see that the wise saying is true, 'Two are better than one.' Up till now your company has been my mercy, and you will have a good return for your labor (cf. Ecclesiastes 4:9-10a)."

"Now then," Christian said, "to prevent drowsiness in this place, let's have a good talk."

"With all my heart," said the other.

"Where shall we begin?" Christian asked.

"Where God began with us," Hopeful replied. "But you begin, if you please."

Christian said, "First I'll sing you a little song:

When saints do sleepy grow, let them come hither,
And hear how these two Pilgrims talk together:
Yes, let them learn from them, in any wise,
So to keep open drowsy, slumb'ring eyes.
Saints' fellowship, if it is managed well
Keeps them awake, and that in spite of hell.

Then Christian began, saying, "I'll ask you a question. How did you first come to think of doing as you're doing now?"

"Do you mean, how did I first come to look after the good of my soul?" asked Hopeful.

"Yes," replied the other. "That's my meaning."

Hopeful began his story. "I continued a good while taking delight in those things that were seen and sold at our fair; things that I believe now would have, if I had continued in them, drowned me in utter ruin and destruction."

"What things are you speaking of?" Christian interjected.

"All the treasures and riches of the world," Hopeful answered. "I took great delight in wild and boisterous behavior, partying, drinking, swearing, lying, immorality, Sabbath-breaking and what-not—all of which tended to destroy the soul. But I found at last, by hearing and considering things that are Divine, which I heard from you and from beloved Faithful, who was put to death for his faith and good life in Vanity Fair, that 'those things result in death' (Romans 6:21–23). And that 'because of such things God's wrath comes on those who are disobedient' (Ephesians 5:6)."

 Hopeful shares the story of how he went from being a citizen of Vanity Fair to a pilgrim on the King's Highway. It didn't happen all at once, he says, but over a period of time he was convicted of his sin and turned to faith.

"And did you fall immediately under the power of this conviction?" Christian asked again.

"No," was the answer, "I wasn't willing at once to know the evil of sin nor the damnation that follows the committing of it. I made a conscious effort instead, when my mind at first began to be shaken by the Word, to shut my eyes against its light."

Christian asked, "But what was the cause of your resistance to the workings of God's blessed Spirit on you at first?"

Hopeful said, "Well, first, I was ignorant that this was the working of God on me. I never thought that by awaking a sinner to the consciousness of sin, God first begins the sinner's conversion. Then, too, sin was still very sweet to my flesh, and I was reluctant to leave it. A third thing that held me back was that I didn't know how to part from my old companions—their presence and actions were still so desirable to me. And finally, the times when convictions were on me were such troublesome and such heart-frightening hours that I couldn't bear so much as the remembrance of them on my heart."

"Then, as it seems, sometimes you got rid of your trouble," his companion observed.

"Yes," he went on, "I did indeed. But it would come into my mind again, and then I would be as bad—no, worse—than I'd been before."

"Why was this?" Christian inquired. "What was it that brought your sins to mind again?"

"Many things," Hopeful said, remembering. "If I met a good person in the streets, or if I heard anyone read from the Bible, or if my head would begin to ache, I would remember. Or if I were told that some of my neighbors were sick, or if I heard the bell toll for someone who had died, or if the thought of dying myself would come to mind, I would remember my sins. If I heard that sudden death had happened to someone else, but especially, when I thought of myself, that I must quickly come to judgment, my sins accused me."

"Did you find that you could at any time with any ease, get rid of the guilt of your sin when by any of these means the conviction of it came on you?" Christian asked.

"No, I didn't. I found that they got hold on my conscience faster, and if I merely thought of going back to sin, it would be double torment to me," Hopeful said.

"So what did you do then?" the other asked.

Hopeful said, "I decided I must try to amend my life. For else, I thought, I'm sure to be damned!"

"And did you try to amend it?" his friend asked.

"Oh, yes," said Hopeful. "I ran in the other direction, not only from my sins but from sinful company, too. I took up religious duties, such as prayer, reading, weeping for sin, speaking truth to my neighbors, and so on. I did these things, and too many others to mention here now."

"And did you think yourself to be well then?" Christian asked.

"Yes, for a while," Hopeful smiled as he spoke. "But, after a time, my trouble came tumbling on me again, and that in spite of all my reformations!"

"But how did that come about, since you were now reformed?" his companion queried.

Hopeful continued: "Well, there were several things that would bring this conviction back upon me, especially such sayings as these: 'All our righteous acts are like filthy rags' (Isaiah 64:6). 'By observing the law no one will be justified' (Galatians 2:16). 'So you also, when you have done everything you were told to do, should say, "We are unworthy servants; we have only done our duty" (Luke 17:10).' And there were many more like these.

"I began to reason with myself like this: If all my righteous acts are like filthy rags; if by observing the law no one will be justified; and if, when we have done everything we were told to do, we are still unworthy, then it is just foolishness to think of heaven according to the law. And then I thought like this: If a person runs ten thousand dollars into debt to a shopkeeper, and after that pays for everything they buy, still, if the old debt stands on the books, for that the shopkeeper can sue them and throw them into prison until they pay the debt."

"Well, and how did you apply this to yourself?" was the next question.

"Why, I thought like this to myself: I have, by my sins, run up a great debt in God's book, and that by reforming now, I can't pay that score. Therefore I should continue to think, in spite of all the changes for the good that I've made in my life, 'But how am I going to get free from the danger of damnation that I've brought on myself through my former transgressions?'"

Hopeful is describing a theory of the atoning work of Jesus Christ known as the "penal substitutionary" theory. It was first explained by Anselm of Canterbury (1033–1109) in his famous book Why a God-Man? *This understanding of Jesus' crucifixion states that due to human sin, God's honor had been insulted; since no human being could be without sin and repair God's honor, God's son had to die to make things right again.*

"A very good application," Christian said. "But please go on."

"Another thing that had troubled me since my overdue changes for the better was that if I looked carefully at the best of what I was now doing, I still saw sin—new sin, mixing itself with the best of what I was doing. So now I was forced to conclude that, notwithstanding my former prideful thoughts concerning myself and my duties, I've committed enough sin in performing one duty to send me to hell, even if my former life had been faultless."

Christian asked, "What did you do then?"

"Do! I couldn't tell what to do," the other exclaimed, "until I opened my mind to Faithful, for he and I became well acquainted. He told me that unless I could obtain the righteousness of a person who had never sinned, neither my own nor all the righteousness of the world could save me."

"And did you think he was telling you the truth?"

Hopeful responded, "If he had told me so when I was pleased and satisfied with my own reformation,

I would have called him a fool for his pains. But now that I had seen my own weakness and the sin that clings to my best performance, I was forced to agree with what he said."

"But did you think, when at first he suggested it to you, that there was such a person to be found, of whom it might justly be said that they never committed sin?" Christian asked.

"I must confess," Hopeful replied, "that the words sounded strange at first; but after a little more talk and company with him I was fully convinced of it."

"And did you ask him who this person was, and how you must be justified by him?"

"Yes, and he told me that it was the Lord Jesus, who dwells at the right hand of the Most High. He told me that I must be justified by Him even by trusting in what He did by Himself during His life, and what He suffered when He hung on the Cross. I asked him further how that person's righteousness could be of such power that it could justify another before God. And he told me that He was the mighty God, and that He did what He did, and also died, not for Himself, but for me; and that what He did and the worthiness of it would be credited to me if I believed in Him" (cf. Hebrews 10, Romans 4, Colossians 1, 1 Peter 1).

Christian spoke again. "What did you do then?"

"I raised objections against my believing, for I thought He wasn't willing to save me," Hopeful said.

"And what did Faithful say to you then?"

"He asked me to go to Him and see," Hopeful said, remembering. "Then I said this was presumption; but he said, no, for I was invited to come (Matthew 11:28). Then he gave me a Book of Jesus, His words, to encourage me the more freely to come; and he said, concerning that Book, that every single word in it stood firmer than heaven and earth (Matthew 24:35). Then I asked him, 'What must I do to come to Him?' And he told me I must make an earnest request on my knees, with all my heart and soul, 'Father, reveal Him to me' (Jeremiah. 29:12-13).

"I asked him further how I ought to make my prayer to Him, and he said, 'Go, and you will find Him on an atonement cover (Exodus 25:17), where He sits all year long, to give pardon and forgiveness to those who come.' I told him that I didn't know what to say when I came. And he told me to say something like this: 'God be merciful to me, a sinner, and make me know and believe in Jesus Christ; for I see that if His righteousness didn't exist, or if I don't have faith in that righteousness, I'm utterly lost. Lord, I've heard that You're a merciful God, and that You've ordained that Your Son Jesus Christ should be the Savior of the world, and that You're willing to present Him as a gift to such a poor sinner as I am, and I am a sinner indeed! Therefore, Lord, take this opportunity and increase Your grace in the salvation of my soul, through Your Son Jesus Christ. Amen' (Hebrews 4:16)."

"And did you do as you were asked?" his companion asked.

"Yes," Hopeful said, "over and over and over."

"And did the Father reveal His Son to you?"

"Not at first, nor at the second, nor at the third, nor at the fourth, nor at the fifth—no, not even at the sixth time, either!" said Hopeful.

"What did you do then?" Christian queried.

"Why, I couldn't tell what to do!" he exclaimed.

"Did you have thoughts of ceasing to pray?" he asked again.

"Yes," was the reply, "several hundred times. The reason I didn't was that I believed that what had been told me was true—that is, that without the righteousness of Christ, the whole world couldn't save me, and therefore, I thought to myself, if I stop I'll die, and all I can do is die at the throne of grace. So with all this, this thought came into my mind, 'Though it linger, wait for it; it will certainly come and will not delay' (Habakkuk 2:3). So I continued praying until the Father showed me His Son."

"How was He revealed to you?" Christian asked eagerly.

Hopeful continued: "I didn't see Him with my bodily eyes, but with the eyes of my understanding (Ephesians 1:18-19). It happened this way: One day I was very sad, I think sadder than at any other time in my life, and this sadness was through a fresh sight of the greatness and depravity of my sins. As I was then looking for nothing but hell and the everlasting damnation of my soul, suddenly, as I was thinking about these things, I saw the Lord Jesus Christ look down from heaven on me, and say, 'Believe in the Lord Jesus Christ, and you will be saved' (Acts 16:31).

"But I replied, 'Lord, I'm a great, a very great sinner.' And He answered, 'My grace is sufficient for you' (2 Corinthians 12:9). Then I said, 'But, Lord, what is believing?' And then I saw from that saying, 'Whoever comes to me will never go hungry, and whoever believes in me will never be thirsty' (John 6:35), that believing and coming are all one; and that whoever comes, that is, runs out in their heart and affections after salvation by Christ, that person indeed believes in Christ.

 This is quite a moving scene, of Jesus appearing to Hopeful, much like Jesus appeared to Saul (renamed, Paul) on the road to Damascus.

Then the tears stood in my eyes, and I asked further, 'But Lord, may such a great sinner as I am be indeed accepted by You, and be saved by You?' And I heard Him say, 'Whoever comes to me I will never drive away' (John 6:37). Then I said, 'But Lord, how must I think of You in order to have the right kind of faith in You?' And He said, 'Christ Jesus came into the world to save sinners' (1 Timothy 1:15). 'Christ is the culmination of the law so that there may be righteousness for every-one who believes' (Romans 10:4). 'He was delivered over to death for our sins, and was raised to life for our justification' (Romans 4:25). He 'loves us and has freed us from our sins by His blood' (Revelation 1:5b). He is 'mediator between God and human beings' (1 Timothy 2:5). 'He always lives to intercede for' us (Hebrews 7:25).

From all these words I gathered that I must look for righteousness in His person, and for repara-tion for my sins by His blood; I understood that what He did in obedience to His Father's law, and in submitting to the penalty of it, was not for Himself but for those who will accept it for their salvation and be thankful. And now my heart was full of joy, my eyes filled with tears, and my affec-tions were running over with love of the name, the people, and the ways of Jesus Christ."

"This was a revelation of Christ to your soul indeed," his brother said. "But tell me particularly what effect this had upon your spirit."

Hopeful said, "It made me see that the whole world, in spite of all its righteousness, is in a state of condemnation. It made me see that God the Father, though He is just, can justly make the repentant sinner righteous. It made me greatly ashamed of the depravity of my former life, and caused me to be distressed with the sense of my own ignorance. For there never came any thought into my heart before now that had so shown me the beauty of Jesus Christ. It made me love a holy life, and long to do something for the honor and glory of the name of the Lord Jesus; yes, I thought that if I had a thousand gallons of blood in my body, I could spill it all for the sake of the Lord Jesus."

Hopeful's Testimony **209**

Chapter Twenty

Christian Talks with Ignorance

I saw then in my dream that Hopeful looked back and saw Ignorance, whom they had left far behind, coming along after them. "Look," he said to Christian, "how far that young man lingers behind us."

"Yes, yes, I see him," Christian said. "He doesn't care for our company."

"But I suppose it wouldn't have hurt him if he had kept pace with us," Hopeful observed.

"True," his friend said, "but I guarantee you he thinks otherwise."

"I think he does," Hopeful said, "but let's wait for him." So they did. Then Christian said to Ignorance, "Come on. Why do you stay so far behind?"

Ignorance replied, "I take pleasure in walking alone a great deal more than in company unless I like the company better."

Then Christian said to Hopeful, under his breath, "Didn't I tell you that he doesn't care for our company?" To Ignorance he said: "Come up, and let's talk away the time in this lonely place.

Come, how are you? How do things stand between God and your soul now?"

"I hope well," the other replied. "For I'm always full of good thoughts that come into my mind to comfort me as I walk."

"What good thoughts? Do tell us," Christian said.

"Why, I think of God and heaven," Ignorance said.

"So do the devils and damned souls," Christian returned. "But I think of them, and desire them," Ignorance said again.

"So do many that are never likely to get there," Christian said. "A sluggard's appetite is never filled" (Proverbs 13:4).

Ignorance wouldn't be put off. "But I think of them and leave everything for them."

Christian shook his head. "That I doubt; for leaving everything is a hard matter. Yes, a harder matter than many people are aware of. But why, or by what, are you persuaded that you've left everything for God and heaven?"

"My heart tells me so," Ignorance replied.

Christian shook his head again. "The wise person says, 'Those who trust in themselves are fools' (Proverbs 28:26)."

"This is speaking of an evil heart, but mine is a good one," said Ignorance.

"But how do you prove that?" Christian asked.

"It comforts me with hopes of heaven," was the reply.

"That may be, through its deceitfulness; for a person's heart may minister comfort to them in the hopes of the thing for which they yet have no ground to hope," Christian went on.

"But my heart and life agree together, and therefore my hope is well grounded," Ignorance answered confidently.

"Who told you that your heart and life agree together?" Christian asked.

"My heart tells me so," Ignorance replied.

Christian exclaimed, "Your heart tells you so! Unless the Word of God bears witness in this matter, no other testimony is of any value."

Ignorance asked, "But isn't a heart good that has good thoughts? And isn't a life good that's according to God's commandments?"

"Yes," the other replied, "a heart is good that has good thoughts, and a life is good that is lived according to God's commandments. But it is one thing indeed to have these, and another thing only to think so."

"Well," Ignorance said, "do tell me what you consider to be good thoughts and a life according to God's commandments."

"There are good thoughts of various kinds," Christian said. "Some concerning ourselves, some concerning God, some concerning Christ, and some concerning other things. Good thoughts concerning ourselves are those that agree with the Word of God."

"And when do our thoughts about ourselves agree with the Word of God?" he asked.

Christian said, "When we pass the same judgment on ourselves that the Word passes. To explain myself: The Word of God says of persons in a natural condition, 'There is no one righteous,' 'there is no one who does good' (Romans 3:10, 12). It also says that 'every inclination of the thoughts of the human heart' is 'only evil all the time' (Genesis 6:5b). And again, 'Every inclination of the human heart is evil from childhood' (Genesis 8:21). Now then, when we think of ourselves in this way, having this realization of it, then our thoughts are good ones, because they're according to the Word of God."

"I'll never believe that my heart is so bad," Ignorance said.

 This is a major point of Calvinist theology, which Puritans like Bunyan followed: the human heart is, by its nature, wicked, depraved, and capable of nothing good on its own. It can only do any good by the grace of God. Ignorance has a hard time swallowing this.

Christian went on, "For this reason you've never had one good thought concerning yourself in your life! But let me go on. As the Word passes judgment on our heart, it also passes judgment on our ways, and when the thoughts of our hearts and ways agree with the judgment that the Word gives of both, then both are good, because they agree with the Word."

"Please make your meaning a little clearer," Ignorance said.

"Why, the Word of God says that human ways are crooked ways (Psalm 125:5)—not good, but devious (Proverbs 2:15)," the other said. "It says they are naturally out of the good way, that they don't know it (Romans 3:17). Now, when a person thinks like this of their ways—when they feel, and with humiliation of heart they think like this, then they have good thoughts about their own ways, because their thoughts now agree with the judgment of the Word of God."

"What are good thoughts concerning God?" Ignorance asked, not desiring to prolong the talk of the human heart and ways.

"Just as I said concerning our thoughts about ourselves, when our thoughts of God agree with what the Word says about Him: and that is, when we think of His being and attributes as the Word has taught—but I can't talk about these things at length now. But we have good thoughts concerning God when we speak of Him with reference to us. When we think that He knows us better than we know ourselves, and can see sin in us when and where we can see none in ourselves. When we think He knows our inmost thought and that our heart, with all its depths, is always open to His eyes. Also when we think that all our righteousness smells horrible in His nostrils, and that He can't abide seeing us standing before Him in any self-confidence, even in all our best performances."

Ignorance was getting angry. "Do you think that I'm such a fool as to think God can see no further than I can? or that I would come to God in the best of my performances?"

"Why, how do you think in this matter?" Christian asked.

"To be brief," Ignorance said, "I think I must believe in Christ for justification."

"How!" Christian exclaimed. "You think you must believe in Christ but you don't see your need of Him! You see neither your original nor present weaknesses, but you have such an opinion of yourself and of what you do that it's plain to see you never saw any necessity of Christ's personal righteousness to justify you before God! How can you say then, 'I believe in Christ'?"

"I believe well enough for all that!" Ignorance retorted.

"How do you believe?" Christian asked.

Ignorance replied, "I believe that Christ died for sinners, and that I'll be justified before God from the curse through His gracious acceptance of my obedience to His law. Or in this way: Christ makes my duties that are religious acceptable to His Father by virtue of His merits, and so I'll be justified."

"Let me give an answer to this confession of your faith," Christian said. "First, you believe with a faith existing only in your imagination, because this faith is nowhere described in the Word. It's the product of your own fantasy.

Here Bunyan is using Christian to counter some of the other understandings of the atonement (Christ's crucifixion and resurrection) that oppose his own Puritan view.

"Second, you believe with a false faith, because your faith takes justification away from the personal righteousness of Jesus Christ, and applies it to your own righteousness.

"Third, your faith doesn't make Christ a justifier of your person, but of your actions, and of your soul because of your right actions, which is false.

"Fourth, this faith is deceitful, and will leave you under punishment for sin in the day of God Almighty. That's because true, justifying faith sets the soul, painfully conscious of its lost condition by the Law, to fleeing for refuge to Christ's righteousness, which is His personal obedience to the law in doing and suffering for us what is required at our hands. This righteousness, I say, true faith accepts as covering the soul, and by it the soul is presented as spotless before God, accepted and declared not guilty of condemnation."

"What!" Ignorance exclaimed again. "Would you have us trust in what Christ in His own person did without us? This opinion of yours would loosen the restraints on our obsessive desires and allow us to live any way we please. What would it matter how we lived, if we may be cleared of our guilt for everything by Christ's personal righteousness, when we believe it?"

"Ignorance is your name," Christian said sadly. "And as is your name, so are you. Even this answer of yours demonstrates what I say. You are ignorant of what justifying righteousness is, and just as ignorant of how to secure your soul through faith in it from the heavy wrath of God. Yes, and you are also ignorant of the true effects of saving faith in this righteousness of Christ, which is to bow and win over the heart of God in Christ, to love His name, His word, His ways and His people—not as you imagine in your ignorance!"

 Ignorance has voiced one of the common complaints about Calvinistic doctrine: if we are justified exclusively by God pre-determination, then we can live any way we want since our actions have nothing to do with our salvation. Christian answers by saying that the mark of a truly predestined person is an inward change of heart and mind that inevitably leads to holy living—known in the Bible as the "fruits of the Spirit."

Hopeful interjected: "Ask him if he ever had Christ revealed to him from heaven."

"What! You are a man for revelations!" Ignorance sneered. "I believe that what both of you and all your kind say about this matter is only the fruit of distracted brains."

"Why, man!" said Hopeful, "Christ is so hidden in God from our natural apprehensions of the flesh that no one can know Him for salvation unless God the Father reveals Him to them."

"That's your faith, but not mine," the other returned. "Yet mine, I have no doubt, is as good as yours, though I don't have as many fanciful ideas in my head as you."

"Allow me to put in a word," Christian said gravely. "You ought not to talk of this matter so lightly. For I'll boldly affirm what my good companion has just said: that no one can know Jesus Christ except by the revelation of the Father (Matthew 11:27). Yes, and faith, too, by which the soul takes hold of Christ, must be brought about by the extreme greatness of His mighty power. But I see, poor Ignorance, that you're ignorant of the working of that faith (Ephesians 1:18-19). Wake up then; see your own wretchedness, and run to the Lord Jesus; and by His righteousness, which is the righteousness of God (for He Himself is God), you'll be delivered from condemnation."

Ignorance said, "You're going so fast I can't keep up your pace. Do go on ahead; I must stay behind for a while."

Then Christian said to Hopeful, "Well, come, my good Hopeful, I see that we must walk by ourselves again."

Chapter Twenty-One

To the Land of Beulah

I saw in my dream that Christian and Hopeful went on ahead, and Ignorance came hobbling after. Christian said to his companion, "I feel very sorry for this poor man, for it will certainly go badly with him at the end." "Yes, yes, I see him," Christian said. "He doesn't care for our company."

"Alas!" Hopeful replied, "there are many others in our town in his condition—whole families, whole streets, even of pilgrims too. And if there are so many in our area, how many do you think there must be in the place where Ignorance was born?"

"Indeed, the Word says, 'He has blinded their eyes, so they cannot see' (cf. John 12:40). But now that we're alone, what do you think of such persons? Do you think that they never have any conviction of sin, and are they never afraid that their state is a dangerous one?" Christian asked.

"I'll let you answer that one," Hopeful replied, smiling, "because you're older than I am."

Christian continued: "Then I say, I think they may sometimes have such convictions and fears.

But, being naturally ignorant, they don't understand that such convictions are for their good; so they desperately attempt to stifle them, and they presumptuously continue to flatter themselves in the way of their own hearts."

Hopeful nodded. "I do believe, as you say, that fear tends to be a very good thing for people, and helps to set them right, especially at the very beginning of their pilgrimage."

"Without all doubt it does, if it's the right kind of fear. 'The fear of the Lord is the beginning of wisdom' (Proverbs 9:10)," Christian said.

"How would you describe what you call 'the right kind of fear'?" Hopeful asked.

Christian replied, "The true or right kind of fear can be identified three ways: first, by its beginning—it's caused by conviction of sin; second, by the fact that it drives the soul to lay hold firmly on Christ for salvation; and third, by its producing and nourishing in the soul a great reverence for God, for His Word and ways, keeping the heart tender and making it afraid to turn from them to the right hand or to the left, to anything that would dishonor God, break the peace of the soul, grieve the Spirit, or give the enemy grounds to lay blame to us."

"Well said," his friend replied. "I believe you've said the truth. Are we now almost out of Enchanted Ground?"

"Why," Christian asked, "are you weary of this line of talk?"

"Not at all," Hopeful replied. "It's only that I'd like to know where we are."

"We have no more than two miles farther to go on Enchanted Ground," Christian said. "But let's return to our subject. Now, the ignorant don't know that the type of conviction that tends to put them in fear is for their good, and therefore they attempt to stifle it."

"How do they do this?" the other asked.

"Well," Christian said, "they think that those fears come from the devil, when in actuality they come from God. Thinking so, they resist them as things that would hurt or destroy them. They also think that these fears spoil their faith, when, alas for them, poor persons that they are, they have no faith at all! So they harden their hearts against these fears. Then they presume they ought not to fear, and, in spite of them, grow presumptuous and over-confident. They see that those fears tend to take away from them their pitiful old self-holiness, and so they resist them with all their might."

"I know something of that myself," said Hopeful. "It was that way with me before I came to know myself."

"Well, we will leave our neighbor Ignorance at this time and take up another profitable question," his friend said.

Hopeful smiled at Christian, "Gladly, but you must still begin."

Christian began: "About ten years ago did you know a man named Temporary in your part of the country who was very prominent in religion then?"

"Know him!" exclaimed Hopeful. "Yes, he lived in Graceless, a town about two miles from Honest, and he lived next door to a fellow named Turnback."

"Right; he lived under the same roof with him," Christian said. "Well that man was wide awake once, I believe, and at that time he had some sight of his sins and the wages that they would bring."

"I agree with you," Hopeful said. "My house is no more than three miles from his, and he would often come to me and talk with many tears. Truly I pitied the man, and was not without hope for him. But one may see that it is not everyone who cries, 'Lord, Lord,' who will enter the kingdom of heaven (Matthew 7:21)."

"He told me once that he was resolved to go on pilgrimage as we go now," the other said, "but all of a sudden he became acquainted with a person named Save-self, and then he became a stranger to me."

"Since you mentioned him, let's think a little about the reason for the sudden backsliding of people like him," Hopeful suggested.

"That might be very good. But in this case, I insist that you begin."

Hopeful spoke without hesitation. "Well then, there are, in my judgment, four reasons for such backsliding.

"First, though the consciences of such persons are awakened, their minds haven't changed. So when the power of guilt wears away, what provoked them to be religious ceases, and they naturally turn to their own ways again (2 Peter 2:22). Since they were eager for heaven only because of a fear of the torments of hell, as soon as that fear subsides, their desire for salvation and heaven also subsides. So it happens that when their guilt and fear are gone, their desire for heaven and happiness dies, and they return to their old ways again.

"Another reason is that they have slavish fears that have mastery over them. I'm speaking now of the fears they have of other people, for 'to fear anyone will prove to be a snare' (Proverbs 29:25). So then, they may seem to be eager for heaven as long as the flames of hell are up to their ears, yet when that terror has subsided a little, they have second thoughts—namely, that it's good to be wise and not to run the hazard of losing everything for something they don't know, or at least, of bringing themselves into unavoidable and unnecessary troubles. And so they fall in line with the world again.

"The embarrassment that accompanies an open profession of faith in Christ is also a block in their way. They're proud and scornful, and religion in their eye is low and contemptible. So, when they've lost their fear of hell and the divine punishment to come, they return again to their old life.

"They can't bear to look at their guilt or think of the terror that lies before them. They prefer to postpone thinking about it, although, perhaps if they were willing, it would make them run for safety to where the righteous run, and be safe there—that is, to Jesus Christ. But because they avoid even the thought of guilt and terror, once they're rid of their awakenings about the God's divine punishment, they harden their hearts gladly and quickly, and choose the kind of ways that will harden them more and more."

"You're pretty close to the truth of it," Christian said. "For the bottom of it all is an unchanged mind and will. Therefore, they're like the criminal who stands before the judge and trembles. He seems to repent most heartily, but the bottom of all is the fear of prison. It's not that he has any hatred of his crime, as is proved when the man is free and steals again—so he's still a criminal. But, if his mind had been changed, he would be otherwise."

Hopeful responded, "Now that I've shown you the reasons why they backslide, will you talk about how they go about backsliding?"

 "Backsliding" is usually used about someone who used to follow Christ but has since fallen away from faith.

Christian said, "So I will, willingly. First, they draw away as many of their own thoughts as possible from any remembrance of God, of death, or of the judgment to come. That's the first step. Then they cast off by degrees their private duties of the inner life—private prayer, curbing their lusts, taking care how they live, sorrow for sin, and the like. Then they avoid the company of lively and warm Christians. After that, they grow cold to their public duty—such as hearing and reading the Word, seeking godly counsel, and the like.

"Then they begin to pick holes, as they say, in some of the godly people—to find fault with them, so that they may have a respectable reason for deserting their own former walk of life. Then they begin to cling to and associate themselves with worldly, loose, and rebellious persons. Then they give way to worldly and lewd, undisciplined talk, jokes, stories, and tidbits of gossip. They're especially glad if they can do this with some who are counted honest, so that they may be made bolder by their example. After this, they begin to play with little sins openly. And then, now that they are hardened, they show themselves as they are. In this way, being launched again into the gulf of misery, unless a miracle of grace stops it, they perish forever in their own deceptions."

By this time, the Pilgrims had gotten over the Enchanted Ground and were entering into the country of Beulah, whose air was very sweet and pleasant. Since their way led directly through it, they were able to find solace there for a time (Isaiah 62:4). Yes, here they continually heard the singing of birds, and every day they saw the flowers appear in the earth, and heard the cooing of doves in the land (Song of Solomon 2:10–12). In this country the sun shines night and day, being beyond the Valley of the Shadow of Death. It was out of reach of Giant Despair, so that they couldn't so much as see Doubting Castle from this land. Here they were within sight of the city to which they were going, and here some of its inhabitants met them, for in this land the Shining Ones commonly walked, because it was upon the borders of heaven.

The name "Beulah" comes from the Old Testament prophet Isaiah—the word means "married," and Isaiah uses it to refer to the new name for God's Promised Land. It's also been used in some more recent hymns and gospel songs to refer to heaven.

In this land, also, the contract between the bride and Bridegroom was renewed: "As a bridegroom rejoices over his bride, so will your God rejoice over you" (Isaiah 62:5). Here they had no lack of grain and wine, for in this place they met with an abundance of what they had been seeking throughout their pilgrimage. Here all the inhabitants of the country called them "the holy people," "the redeemed of the Lord," and "the sought-out ones."

Now, as they walked in this land, they had more rejoicing than they'd had when they were farther away from the Kingdom to which they were headed. Drawing near the city, they had a more perfect view of it. It was built of pearls and precious stones, and the street of it was paved with gold, so that by the natural glory of the city and the reflection of the sunbeams on it, Christian fell sick with desire for it. Hopeful, too, had an attack of sickness once or twice. So there they lay for a while, crying out because of their pangs: "If you find my beloved, tell him I am faint with love" (Song of Solomon 5:8).

But, being strengthened a little, and better able to bear their sickness, they walked on their way, and came nearer and nearer to it. There they found orchards, vineyards, and gardens, whose gates opened into the highway. As they came up to these places, the gardener stood in the road, and the Pilgrims asked, "Whose lovely vineyards and gardens are these?" He answered, "They're the King's, and they're planted here for His own delight and for the help of pilgrims." So they were invited into the vineyards and told to refresh themselves and eat their fill (Deuteronomy 23:24). The gardener also showed them the King's walks, and the arbors where He delighted to be; and here they stayed and slept.

Now I saw in my dream that they talked more in their sleep at this period than they had ever done in their entire journey. I wondered at this, but the gardener said to me, "Why do you wonder at the matter? It's the nature of the fruit of the grapes of these vineyards to go down so sweetly as to cause the lips of those who are asleep to speak."

When they awoke, they prepared themselves to go up to the City. But, as I said, the reflection of the sun on the City was so extremely glorious that they couldn't, as yet, look straight at it [(for "the city was pure gold" (Revelation 21:18)], so they had to look through an instrument made for that purpose (2 Corinthians 3:18). I saw that, as they went on, they were met by two beings in clothing that shone like gold, and whose faces shone as the light.

These beings asked the Pilgrims where they came from, and they told them. They also asked them where they had lodged, and what difficulties and dangers, what comforts and pleasures they had met in the Way, and they told them.

Then the beings who met them said, "You have just two more difficulties to meet with, and then you will be in the City."

Christian then, and his companion, asked the beings to go along with them, and they agreed to do this. "But," they said, "you must obtain it by your own faith."

So I saw in my dream that they went on together until they came in sight of the gate.

Chapter Twenty-Two

The Final Conflict

Now I saw that between the Pilgrims and the gate to the Celestial City lay a River, but there was no bridge to go over, and the River was very deep. At the sight of it, the Pilgrims were stunned, but the persons who went with them said, "You must go through, or you cannot come to the gate." "Alas!" Hopeful replied, "there are many others in our town in his condition—whole families, whole streets, even of pilgrims too. And if there are so many in our area, how many do you think there must be in the place where Ignorance was born?"

☞ *Even in ancient Greek mythology, the afterworld was surrounded by a river, Styx, which circles Hades nine times. Souls who wanted to pass had to be transported by the ferryman, Phlegethon.*

The Pilgrims then began to inquire if there was no other way to the gate, to which the persons answered, "Yes, but only two, Enoch (Genesis 5:24) and Elijah (2 Kings 2:11), have been permitted to tread that path since the foundation of the world, and no others will until the last trumpet sounds" (1 Corinthians 15:51-52). The Pilgrims then, especially Christian, began to worry in their minds, and they looked this way and that, but no way could be found by which they might escape the River. Then they asked the persons if the waters were all of the same depth. They said, "No," yet they couldn't help them in that case. "For," said they, "you'll find it deeper or shallower according to the depth of your belief in the King of the place."

The Pilgrims then descended to the water, and entering it, Christian began to sink. Crying out to his good friend, Hopeful, he said, "I'm sinking in the deep waters; the engulfing waves are going over my head; all his waves are going over me! (cf. Jonah 2:5)."

Then Hopeful said, "Be of good cheer, my brother. I feel the bottom and it's good!"

Then Christian said, "Ah! my friend, 'the cords of death entangled me' (Psalm 116:3); I won't see the land that flows with milk and honey."

With that, great darkness and horror fell upon Christian, so he couldn't see in front of him. Here he also in great measure lost his senses, so that he could neither remember nor talk in an orderly way about the sweet refreshments that he had met with in the way of his pilgrimage. But all the words that he spoke continued to reveal that he had an intense fear in his mind and in his heart that he would die in that River and never obtain entrance at the gate.

Here, also, as those who stood by him were aware, he was greatly troubled at thoughts of the sins that he had committed, both before and after he became a Pilgrim. It was observed that he was troubled with apparitions of hobgoblins and evil spirits, because every now and then, what he said he would indicate that. Therefore, Hopeful had much to do to keep his brother's head above water. In fact, sometimes he would be quite out of sight, and then he would rise up again half dead. Hopeful would also try to comfort him, saying, "Brother, I see the gate and people standing by to receive us"; but Christian would answer, "It is you, it is you they're waiting for. You've been Hopeful ever since I knew you."

"And so have you," the other said.

"Ah, brother!" Christian said, "surely if I was right He would now arise and help me; but for my sins He has brought me into the trap and left me."

Then Hopeful said, "My brother, you've quite forgotten the text where it is said of the wicked, 'They have no struggles; their bodies are healthy and strong. They are free from common human burdens; they are not plagued by human ills' (Psalm 73:4-5). These troubles and distresses that you're going through in these waters are no sign that God has forsaken you. They're sent to test you, to see whether you'll call to mind what, prior to this, you've received of His goodness and live on Him in your distresses."

Then I saw in my dream that Christian was as though lost in thought for a while. Then Hopeful added this word, "Be of good cheer. Jesus Christ is making you well!" With that, Christian spoke out with a loud voice, "Oh, I see Him again! And He's telling me, 'When you pass through the waters, I will be with you; and when you pass through the rivers, they will not sweep over you' (Isaiah 43:2)."

Then they both took courage, and after that the enemy was as still as a stone, until they had gotten across. Soon Christian found ground to stand on, and so it followed that the rest of the River was only shallow. So they got over.

Now on the bank of the River, on the other side, they saw the two Shining Ones again, who were waiting for them there. As the Pilgrims came out of the River, the Shining Ones said to them, "We are ministering spirits, sent to serve those who will inherit salvation" (Hebrews 1:14). And so they went along toward the gate.

 Throughout history, there have been many depictions of heaven, in art, movies, songs, and literature. Bunyan ends his tale with a beautiful description of that most beautiful eternal place.

Now you must note that the City stood on a mighty hill, but the Pilgrims went easily up that hill, because they had these two beings to lead them up by the arms. Also, they had left their mortal garments behind them in the River, for though they went in with them, they came out without them. Therefore, they went up with great agility and speed, even though the foundation on which the City was placed was higher than the clouds. Therefore, they went up through the regions of the air, sweetly talking as they went, and greatly comforted because they had arrived safely over the River, and because they had such glorious companions to accompany them.

The talk they had with the Shining Ones was about the glory of the place. They told them that the beauty and glory of the City were inexpressible. "There," they said, "is Mount Zion, the heavenly Jerusalem, thousands upon thousands of angels in joyful assembly, and the spirits of the righteous made perfect (Hebrews 12:22–24). You're going now to the paradise of God, in which you will see the Tree of Life, and eat of its never-fading fruits. When you come there, you will have white robes given you, and your walk and talk will be every day with the King, yes, all the days of eternity.' There you'll never again see such things as you saw when you were in the lower region on the earth—sorrow, sickness, affliction, and death, 'for the old order of things has passed away' (Revelation 21:4). You're going to Abraham, to Isaac, and to Jacob and to the prophets—persons whom God has taken away to be spared from evil. Those who walk uprightly enter into peace; they find rest as they lie in death" (Isaiah 57:1-2).

"What must we do in the holy place?" asked the Pilgrims.

The answer came, "There you must receive the comforts of all your labor and have joy for all your sorrow; you must reap what you have sown, yes, the fruit of all your prayers and tears and sufferings for the King throughout your pilgrimage (Galatians 6:7). In that place you must wear crowns of gold, and enjoy the perpetual sight and vision of the Holy One, for there you 'shall see Him as he is' (1 John 3:2).

"There also you'll serve Him continually with praise, with shouts of thanksgiving, Whom you desired to serve in the world, though with much difficulty, because of the weakness of your body. There your eyes will be delighted with seeing and your ears with hearing the pleasant voice of the Mighty One. There you will enjoy your friends again who have gone on before you. And there you will with joy receive everyone who follows into the holy place after you. There you'll also be clothed with glory and majesty and put into a chariot fit to ride out with the King of Glory. On the Day when He comes with sound of trumpet in the clouds, as on the wings of the wind, you'll come with Him (1 Thessalonians 4:13–17). When he sits on the throne of judgment, you'll sit by Him. Yes, and when He passes sentence on all the workers of iniquity, whether angels or humans, you'll also have a voice in that judgment, because they were His enemies and yours (Jude 14-15). Also, when He returns again to the City, you'll go, too, with the sound of the trumpet, and you'll be with Him forever."

Now, while they were drawing toward the gate in this manner, a company of the heavenly armies came out to meet them. To the company, the two Shining Ones said, "These are the persons who have loved our Lord when they were in the world and who left everything for His holy name. He sent us to bring them, and we've brought them this far on their desired journey, so that they may go in and look their Redeemer in the face with joy."

Then the heavenly army gave a great shout, saying, "Blessed are those who are invited to the wedding supper of the Lamb!" (Revelation 19:9). At this time there also came out to meet them several of the King's trumpeters dressed in white and shining clothing. They made the heavens echo with their loud and melodious sounds. These trumpeters saluted Christian and Hopeful with ten thousand welcomes from the world; and they did this with shouting and the sound of the trumpet.

Then they surrounded the Pilgrims on all sides. Some went in front of them, some behind, some on the right hand, some on the left, as if to guard them through the upper regions. And as they went, they made the heavens resound with melodious music. It looked as though heaven itself had come down to meet them. So therefore they walked on together, and as they walked, the trumpeters continued their music, while with gestures of welcome and singing the army let them know how glad they were to have them in their company and with what joy they had come out to meet them.

For the two Pilgrims, it was as though they were in heaven before they came to the gate, so swallowed up they were with the sight of the angels and the singing of the heavenly army. Here, too, they had the City itself in view, and they thought they heard all the bells in it ringing to welcome them to it. But above all was the warm and joyful thought they had about their own living there with such a company as this—forever and ever. Oh, what voice or pen could express their glorious joy! And so they came up to the gate.

Now when they had arrived at the gate of the City, there were written over it in letters of gold, "Blessed are those who wash their robes, that they may have the right to the tree of life and may go through the gates into the city" (Revelation 22:14).

Then I saw in my dream that the Shining Ones told them to knock at the gate, which they did. Some came and looked over the gate at them, namely, Enoch, Moses, and Elijah, and several others. It was said to them, "These Pilgrims have come from the City of Destruction for the love that they bear for the King of this place." Then each of the Pilgrims gave over his certificate that he had received at the beginning of his journey. Then the certificates were carried in to the King, who when He had read them said, "Where are these men?"

"They are standing outside the gate," was the answer.

The King then commanded them to open the gate, "that the righteous nation may enter," He said, "the nation that keeps faith" (Isaiah 26:2).

Now I saw in my dream that these two men went in at the gate. And as they entered, they were transfigured, and they had clothing put on them that shone like gold. They also received harps and crowns—the harps to praise continually, and the crowns in token of honor.

Then I heard in my dream that all the bells in the City rang again for joy, and that it was said to the Pilgrims:

COME AND SHARE YOUR MASTER'S HAPPINESS (Matthew 25:21, 23).

I also heard the men themselves, singing with a loud voice, saying,

TO HIM WHO SITS ON THE THRONE AND TO THE LAMB BE PRAISE AND HONOR AND GLORY AND POWER, FOR EVER AND EVER! (Revelation 5:13b)

Now, just as the gates were opened to let in the men, I looked in after them, and the City shone like the sun; the streets also were paved with gold, and in the streets many persons walked with crowns on their heads, palms in their hands, and golden harps for singing praises.

Some that I saw had wings, and they answered one another without ceasing, saying, "Holy, holy, holy is the Lord" (Isaiah 6:3). And after that, they shut the gates. And when I had seen all this, I wished that I were among them.

Chapter Twenty-Three

A Concluding Warning

Now, while I was gazing on all these things, I turned my head to look back, and I saw Ignorance coming up to the riverside. But he soon got over, and did so without half the difficulty that the other two Pilgrims had met with. For it happened that there was then in that place a ferryman named Vain-hope, who with his boat helped him over. So he, like the others I had seen, went up the hill to come up to the gate. But he came alone, and no one met him with the least encouragement. When he had arrived at the gate, he looked up to the writing that was above it, and then began to knock, supposing that he would quickly be given entrance. But he was asked by the persons who looked over the top of the gate, "Where did you come from, and what are you looking for?"

 Well, I guess that John Bunyan didn't want to end his tale with a picture of heaven—instead, we get one more warning as Ignorance is pitched out of a door and down to hell.

He answered, "I ate and drank with the King, and He taught in our streets" (cf. Luke 13:26).

Then they asked him for his certificate, that they might go in and show it to the King; so he fumbled in his chest pocket for one, but didn't find one.

Then they said, "Do you not have a certificate?"

But the man answered not a word.

So they told the King, but He refused to come down to see him. Instead, he commanded the two Shining Ones who had led Christian and Hopeful to the City to go out and take Ignorance, and tie him hand and foot, and take him away. Then they tied him up, and carried him through the air, to the door that I saw in the side of the hill, and put him in there.

Then I saw that there was a way to hell, even from the very gates of heaven, as well as from the City of Destruction!

So I awoke, and saw that it was a dream.

The Author's Conclusion

Now, Reader, I have told my dream to thee;
See if thou canst interpret it to me,
Or to thyself, or neighbor; but take heed
Of misinterpreting; for that, instead
Of doing good, will but thyself abuse:
By misinterpreting, evil ensues.
Take heed also, that thou be not extreme
In playing with the outside of my dream:
Nor let my figure or similitude
Put thee into a laughter or a feud.
Leave this for boys and fools; but as for thee,
Do thou the substance of my matter see?
Put by the curtains, look within my veil,
Turn up my metaphors, and do not fail
There, if thou seekest them, such things find
As will be helpful to an honest mind.
What of my dross thou findest there, be bold
To throw away, but yet preserve the gold;
What if my gold be wrapped up in ore?—
None throws away the apple for the core.

But if thou shalt cast all away as vain,
I know not but 'twill make me dream again.

About Paraclete Press

Who We Are

Paraclete Press is an ecumenical publisher of books and recordings on Christian spirituality. Our publishing represents a full expression of Christian belief and practice—from Catholic to Evangelical, from Protestant to Orthodox.

Paraclete Press is the publishing arm of the Community of Jesus, an ecumenical monastic community in the Benedictine tradition. As such, we are uniquely positioned in the marketplace without connection to a large corporation and with informal relationships to many branches and denominations of faith.

We like it best when people buy our books from booksellers, our partners in successfully reaching as wide an audience as possible.

What We Are Doing

Books

Paraclete Press publishes books that show the richness and depth of what it means to be Christian. Although Benedictine spirituality is at the heart of all that we do, we publish books that reflect the Christian experience across many cultures, time periods, and houses of worship.

We publish books that nourish the vibrant life of the church and its people—books about spiritual practice, formation, history, ideas, and customs.

We have several different series of books within Paraclete Press, including the bestselling Living Library series of modernized classic texts; A Voice from the Monastery—giving voice to men and women monastics about what it means to live a spiritual life today; award-winning literary faith fiction; and books that explore Judaism and Islam and discover how these faiths inform Christian thought and practice.

Recordings

From Gregorian chant to contemporary American choral works, our music recordings celebrate the richness of sacred choral music through the centuries. Paraclete is proud to distribute the recordings of the internationally acclaimed choir Gloriæ Dei Cantores, who have been praised for their "rapt and fathomless spiritual intensity" by *American Record Guide*, and the Gloriæ Dei Cantores Schola, which specializes in the study and performance of Gregorian chant. Paraclete is also the exclusive North American distributor of the recordings of the Monastic Choir of St. Peter's Abbey in Solesmes, France, long considered to be a leading authority on Gregorian chant performance.

Learn more about us at our Web site:
www.paracletepress.com,
or call us toll-free at
1-800-451-5006.

You Converted Me

The Confessions of St. Augustine
Introduction and Notes by Tony Jones
Modernized Translation by Robert J. Edmonson, CJ
ISBN: 1-55725-463-X
232 pages
$16.95, Trade paper

"A boy grows into a man, getting into the kind of mischief that a lot of boys do (messing around with girls, stealing, getting in trouble at school). Meanwhile, his over-protective Christian mother prays fervently for the salvation of his soul. . . ."

So begins the introduction to one of the most famous true stories of all time. This young man, born in 354, became one of the greatest heroes for God in all of history. In these pages, Augustine tells all – from the deep trust he had in his mother, to his guilt over stealing from a neighbor, to his dramatic conversion at age thirty-three.

"*You Converted Me* makes Augustine's classic *Confessions* accessible and available to readers today - young or old, religious or not."
—Brian McLaren, author/activist

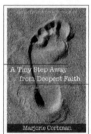

A Tiny Step Away from Deepest Faith

A Teenager's Search for Meaning
Marjorie Corbman
ISBN:1-55725-429-X
101 pages
$9.95, Trade paper

In this passionate search for God, love, and identity, Marjorie Corbman dismantles the misconceptions surrounding today's teenagers. Marjorie charts her own transformations, from growing up in a home with little interest in spiritual things to her own preparations for conversion. Along the way, she discusses intimacy, tradition, eternity, community, justice, escape, and faith.

"I was a youth pastor for ten years, and I've read lots of teenagers' reflections on God and faith. Never have I seen so articulate and moving a work of spiritual memoir from a teenager as Marjorie Corbman's. She writes with beauty and insight beyond her years. Her writing is yet more evidence that there is, indeed, a loving God."
—Tony Jones, author of *The Sacred Way* and *Postmodern Youth Ministry*

Available from most booksellers or through Paraclete Press:
www.paracletepress.com
1-800-451-5006 • Try your local bookstore first.